MAIN SIGHTS

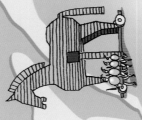

⑥ **Troy** Site of a legendary Greek victory, involving the army and a large wooden horse

THRACE

Lesbos

② **Kos** The island where Hippocrates has set up his medical school

The gold and ivory statue of Athene stands in her temple on the **Acropolis**.

MAP OF ANCIENT GREECE

CHALCIDICE

Aegean Sea

⑩ **Mount Olympus**

Home of the gods when they're not out causing trouble elsewhere

Selling fresh fish

The area shaded in green shows the extent of Greek colonization.

MACEDONIA

𝒩

THESSALY

⑤ **Delphi**

Home of the famous oracle, who can answer any question you care to ask

Zeus, king of the gods, feeling grumpy

The Pythia (oracle at Delphi) having a vision

ATTICA

Piraeus Port of Athens and home to traders from everywhere ③

① **Athens** The city-state with everything, including an enormous statue of Athene

A trireme (Greek warship)

Mycenae

④ **Olympia**

See the original Olympics here.

ARCADIA

Argos

⑦ **Laurion** Site of the ancient world's largest silver mines

⑨ **Delos** Island-hoppers should stop off here where the Delian League (an alliance of Greek states) met for the first time.

MESSENIA

⑧ **Sparta**

Home of the scary Spartans: for information only. <u>DON'T</u> visit!

A Spartan warrior keeping his slave hard at it

PELOPONNESE

Unlike merchant ships, triremes have oars as well as sails.

Mediterranean Sea

A merchant ship setting off to trade silver for silk and spices

Crete Island home of the fabled Minotaur

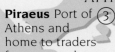

First published in 2003 by Usborne Publishing Ltd., Usborne House, 83-85 Saffron Hill, London EC1N 8RT, England. www.usborne.com Copyright © 2003, 1989,1982 Usborne Publishing Ltd.

A VISITOR'S GUIDE TO
ANCIENT GREECE

Lesley Sims

**Designed & illustrated
by Ian McNee**

Additional illustrations by Ian Jackson, Inklink-Firenze
Edited by Jane Chisholm

History consultant: Dr. Anne Millard

CONTENTS

Internet links
If you're not up to taking an actual trip to Ancient Greece, why not take a virtual tour instead? Go to **www.usborne-quicklinks.com** and type the keywords "guide to ancient greece".

A BRIEF BACKGROUND

Greece, its beaches lapped by the sparkling Mediterranean Sea, is an idyllic destination. Combine it with a trip into the past and you're sure of a fun visit. This guide, aimed at the first-time visitor to Ancient Greece, has all the information any tourist through time needs to know.

It begins with a quick run down of Ancient Greece through the ages. (If you're not that interested in history, turn the page for details of what to pack and who to avoid on your trip.)

Where you'll find Greece in Europe

Greece is a mountainous country in southern Europe bordered on three sides by the Mediterranean Sea.

IN THE BEGINNING

1. Almost 40,000 years ago and people were already around.
2. Civilization arrives some time later. By 2000BC, the Minoans are living it up on Crete. But that lasts barely a millennium (1,000 years).
3. 1600BC and it's the turn of a people called the Mycenaeans to dominate mainland Greece.
4. But, only 400 years later, they're destroyed by war and famine.

> **A WORD OF WARNING!**
> You'll be greeted by blank looks if you ask for anything Greek. Greece won't be known as Greece until the Romans arrive. At the time of your visit it's called *Hellas* and the Greeks are *Hellenes*.

THEN

5. The Dark Ages hit, not for the Greeks but us (because we're in the dark about what was going on).
6. After 300 years of darkness, the "Archaic Period" begins: people write and paint again – leaving us masses of useful evidence about their lives – and travel becomes popular.
7. The country is divided into independent city-states (each one known as a *polis*), ruled by aristocrats or sometimes one man, called a "tyrant".

Hitching a lift on the bandwagon to Athens

NOW

8. The "Classical Period" dawns and it's a Golden Age. It only lasts from 500-336BC, so time your visit to make the most of it.
9. The city of Athens grows to dominate all the other city-states. Between 479-431BC, everyone who's anyone visits Athens.
Ready to join them?

SETTING THE SCENE

The best time to visit is between 479 and 431BC. Greece (*Hellas*) is buzzing. Trade is flourishing, cities are rich and the city-state of **Athens**, in particular, is at the forefront of an art explosion. When you join the cream of dramatists, philosophers, and sculptors heading to Greece, you'll see for yourself what an inspirational country it is.

TOP OF THE POLS

The man in charge is Pericles, who will dominate Athenian politics from 443-429BC. He's famed for his dignity, eloquence and – in the age of the backhander – his incorruptibility.

VISA INFORMATION

If your heart sinks at the thought of a long wait at an embassy, cheer up. You won't need a visa or passport. Greece is a cosmopolitan country welcoming foreign visitors. But don't outstay that welcome. After a month, resident "aliens" must register and pay taxes.

WEATHER

Greece has rainy winters but long hot summers. Ideally, try to visit in late spring or early summer – unless you want to include a trip to **Olympia** for the Olympics (see pages 36-37). The games don't begin until the very end of June.

WHAT TO PACK

Bed: If you have a light tent and sleeping bag, it's not a bad idea to bring them with you. Camping is often a tourist's only option and you won't need extra blankets if you visit during the warmer months.

Board: Bring food since, even if you do find an inn, they don't provide bed *and* breakfast. A water bottle is also useful. There are plenty of wells and fountains around. You'll need to keep up your liquid intake or you'll risk dehydration – and there are no canned drink alternatives.

Clothes: Your best plan is to buy a Greek tunic from a market on arrival. To protect against the sun and dust, you'll find a broad brimmed hat, and a riding cloak (called a *chlamys*) are perfect.

Currency: Pick this up there too, but bring a good supply of spices. You'll need to trade them for your first batch of coins. Some places also accept spices instead of cash. Coins tend to be silver, decorated with hero or animal motifs. You're most likely to use *drachmas* and *obols* (1/6 drachma). The only minor annoyance is that each city-state issues its own coins.*

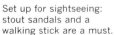

Set up for sightseeing: stout sandals and a walking stick are a must.

4

DOs & DON'Ts

The Ancient World is a conventional place and Greece is no exception. To make the most of your stay, read and remember these tips. They won't only save your blushes, they could save you from arrest.

Cleanliness: To be sure of fitting in, you can't just be clean, but super clean. If there's no bathroom where you're staying, make sure you become a regular at the local baths.

Scraping off oil (used in place of soap)

His 'n' hers: If you're visiting in a mixed group, be prepared to split up. At home, men and women live in separate rooms and they lead pretty much separate lives. Men dominate society, in public at least, and gender discrimination is a fact of life. Whether it's something you've grown up with or not, here you'll just have to get used to it.

Most women have sheltered existences and married women from rich families rarely leave home at all. To avoid embarrassment, activities which are strictly all male are indicated by the following symbol:

Males only

With friends like those... Watch what company you keep. Hang with rowdy companions, you'll get a bad reputation and could be deported.

QUIRKY QUOTES

For a deeper understanding of the place and people, some pages have quotes from visitors to Ancient Greece or famous locals. Quotes are shown like this:

> " *The quotes give useful insights but they are personal opinions which don't necessarily reflect the viewpoints of the writers of this guide.* "

TOURIST TIPS

Finally, on most pages, you'll find extra hints for things to do and how to behave, shown like this:

TOP TIPS FOR TOURISTS

No. 1: Don't mention the war!

Your first and crucial piece of advice: don't mention the Persians. They invaded in 480BC, destroying the holiest temples in their excitement, and were only defeated a year later. If you visit soon after – 478BC say – you'll see it's (understandably) still a touchy subject.

ATHENS & THE ACROPOLIS

If you're like most visitors, you'll make **Athens** your first stop. With the recent boom in art and trade, it's a very good place to start. The city is dominated by the **Acropolis** (its name means "high ground"), the rocky hill where the Athenians first settled.

As the city expanded, houses and shops were built around the base of the hill. The Acropolis was left as you'll see it today, a sanctuary for temples and shrines.

To help you get your bearings, the picture below shows the layout of the city. The smaller plan is to guide you around the Acropolis itself. Bear in mind, though, that if you come earlier than 437BC, not all of the temples are finished – or even there.

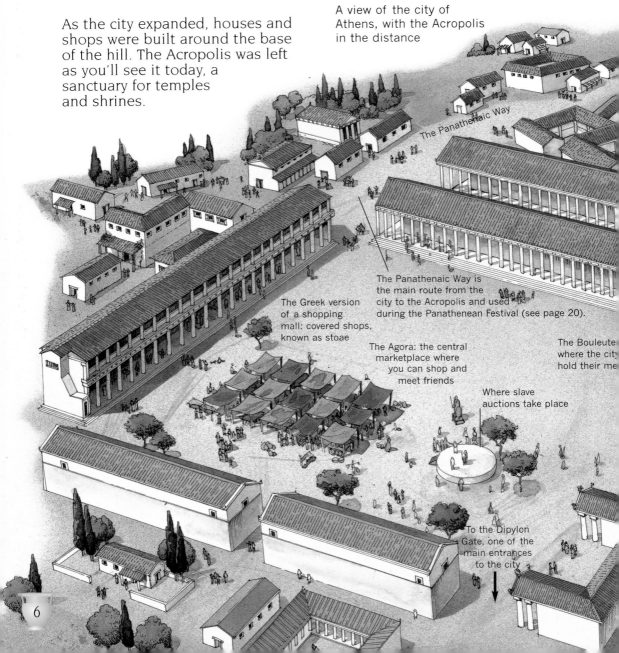

A view of the city of Athens, with the Acropolis in the distance

The Panathenaic Way

The Panathenaic Way is the main route from the city to the Acropolis and used during the Panathenean Festival (see page 20).

The Greek version of a shopping mall: covered shops, known as stoae

The Agora: the central marketplace where you can shop and meet friends

Where slave auctions take place

The Bouleute where the city hold their me

To the Dipylon Gate, one of the main entrances to the city

The Acropolis

A close-up of the Acropolis

Propylaia: gateway to the Acropolis and art gallery (c.437BC)

Temple of Erechtheion (c.421BC)

The Parthenon, a temple currently being rebuilt by Pericles

Temple of Athena Nike (c.424BC)

Statue of Athena (visible out at sea)

Sanctuary of Artemis

Arena of Dionysus

The circular Tholos, where council leaders meet

TOP TIPS FOR TOURISTS

No. 2: The city at your feet

To get a feel of the place when you arrive, head straight for the Acropolis. It's the best place to get a view over the entire city. (It's also a useful landmark to keep in sight when exploring the streets below.)

Where the majority of craftsmen live and work

A temple dedicated to Hephaestos, god of metalsmiths and craftsmen. (Locals call it the Theseum.)

7

WHERE TO STAY

Most tourists stay with friends or relatives en route to their destination. But this isn't really an option for a time tourist (unless you speak fluent Ancient Greek and make friends quickly).

As the weather stays warm for most of the year, why not join the locals and camp out? In towns, people happily sleep under the porches of public buildings. There are no worries here of being moved along with the sarcastic comment, "Haven't you got a home to go to?"

A guard outside a hotel: hotels are very exclusive, largely catering for the very rich and famous.

HOTELS

The largest towns have hotels, called *katagogia*, and it's always worth trying to book into one, just for the experience. If they're not booked up – and you're persuasive – you may be able to talk your way in. On the whole, though, *katagogia* are reserved for VIPs. Humble tourists are shown the door.

Slaves' rooms

Bathroo

Kitchen: slaving over a hot stove

Lifting the roof off: inside a Greek house

Altar

Lobby

A potter's workshop

HOME SWEET HOME

If camping isn't for you, you may be able to rent rooms in a private house. Think yourself lucky if you get to stay in a house the size of the one above. Most are much smaller, though with similar rooms. Many also have a central courtyard, with the rooms facing in. (People here have a thing about privacy.)

Since only larger houses have space to rent rooms, you can be sure of comfortable surroundings. There may even be a bakery on the ground floor, so you won't have far to walk for your pastries. House rules are few, but remember: never go near the women's quarters without being invited. Trespass and you risk the wrath (and fists) of your landlord.

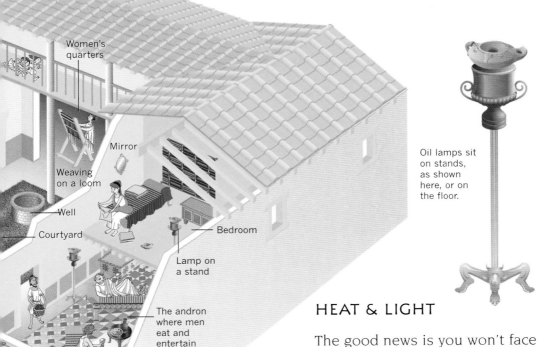

Women's quarters

Mirror

Weaving on a loom

Well

Courtyard

Bedroom

Lamp on a stand

The andron where men eat and entertain

Statue of god Hermes, to protect house

Oil lamps sit on stands, as shown here, or on the floor.

HEAT & LIGHT

The good news is you won't face an electricity bill at the end of your stay. The bad news? There's no electricity. This means relying on oil lamps and rooms aren't that well-lit. If you've ever read by candlelight, you'll know the more wicks the better. It is a gentler light though, making for cosy evenings. If you're cold, you could borrow a brazier (a metal container on a stand in which you burn charcoal).

FURNITURE

There's not a great deal of furniture and it's mostly wooden – elaborately carved and inlaid with ivory, silver and gold in wealthier households. The master of the house sits on a *thronos* (fancy chair); women have smaller chairs. You'll probably have to make do with a stool. But eating is done lying down (on couches), and tables are low, to slide under the couches when not in use. Beds have sheets, a mattress and pillows, so you should at least have a good night's sleep.

Thronos

Most tables are three-legged.

TOP TIPS FOR TOURISTS

No. 3: Burglar alarm!

Houses are built of wood and mud bricks which have been hardened in the sun. This makes their walls very easy to tunnel through – as many homeowners know to their cost. So, when you go out, take your valuables with you. Better yet, don't bring them away with you in the first place.

WHAT TO EAT

Ancient Greece is an ideal destination for healthy-eaters, not to mention vegetarians. Most people live on – "enjoy" isn't really the word – a diet of barley porridge. This is livened up with bread, cheese, eggs and plenty of fruit and vegetables.

If you can't live without meat, be sure to bring enough spices to trade with. Only the wealthy can eat meat every day. But for the rich, there's the usual choice of lamb, pork and poultry, plus goat. You'll even find beef – though there's very little grazing land to raise cows, which makes beef even more costly. You might want to wait until the end of the trip before blowing the last of your budget on that large steak.

THE MAIN MEAL

You may have heard the expression, "Breakfast like a king, dine like a pauper." Well, the Greeks live it in reverse. (Except for the poor, who eat like paupers all the time.) With breakfast simply a little bread soaked in wine and lunch a light snack, everyone builds up an appetite for dinner.

CHEERS!

The most common drink is wine, always diluted with water and mixed in a vast container, or *krater*. If that's not for you, quench your thirst at one of the many public fountains.

Kraters can be huge. Some are the size of a large dog.

OLIVES

Olives or their oil turn up in almost every Greek dish in some form or other. Olives are pressed several times over for the different grades of oil, which is used for medicine and fuel, as well as cooking. The best oil (the one used in cooking) comes from the first pressing.

An olive press

TOP TIPS FOR TOURISTS

No. 4: Catch of the day

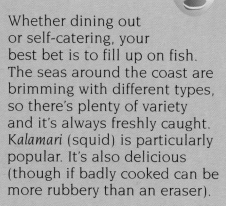

Whether dining out or self-catering, your best bet is to fill up on fish. The seas around the coast are brimming with different types, so there's plenty of variety and it's always freshly caught. *Kalamari* (squid) is particularly popular. It's also delicious (though if badly cooked can be more rubbery than an eraser).

DINNER PARTIES

Luckily for the male tourist, the Greeks don't like eating alone, so invitations to dinner are frequent. You could also be taken along as a friend of a guest. Women and young children eat in a separate room, except at private family occasions.

Everyone reclines on cushions to eat and many diners bring their own. The most important guest is seated on the host's right. You can tell how popular you are by how close you're sitting to the host.

The courses are endless: fish, meat and vegetable dishes, cheeses, nuts and pastries. But food is incidental to the main business of the evening – drinking and the after-dinner discussion (see pages 16-17).

> **"** *In some parts they call a sumptuous banquet, "Having a bite to eat."* **"**
>
> **Socrates, a philosopher**

PARTY ETIQUETTE

Dress smartly and arrive on time. The other diners won't wait. Slaves will rinse and perfume your feet at the door. (If you've spent all day on foot, sightseeing, the slaves will be grateful if you've washed them first.)

They'll also bring water for you to rinse your hands. You'll mostly eat with your fingers, though there are spoons. But don't look for napkins. Instead, guests wipe their hands on a special paste. (Don't eat it by mistake!)

If you arrive late, the best seats may have gone.

You can enjoy live music while you eat.

Just wave a hand to have your cup refilled.

The food is brought in, already laid out on tables.

Male diners are entertained with the witty chat of professional female companions.

A dinner party getting under way

GETTING AROUND

Try to avoid war zones.

Greece's spectacular mountains make for great views, but they're not such fun when it comes to getting around. The country's hilly terrain makes travel hard going, and most of the decent roads tend to lead to the religious sites. Fine if these are on your itinerary, but not much help if you're "templed" out.

The busiest routes have reasonable roads. Rivers have few bridges, but water levels are low in the summer so this shouldn't be a problem. But you'll face long hold-ups if you travel in winter, as chariots and carts continually get stuck in mud.

Try to travel light: unless you can afford a mule to carry your backpack, you'll be lugging it on foot. If walking isn't for you, buy a horse and perhaps a carriage. You can always sell them on at the end of your stay. But you'll need plenty of money. Horses are expensive because there are so few places with enough pasture to feed them.

You won't get saddle sore. There are no saddles.

Most people walk everywhere, often carrying a walking stick and folding stool. Don't laugh. Within a day, you'll follow their example. The stick helps on the rough ground and the stool is a godsend – there are no handy roadside coffee stops. Another vital accessory is a torch (of the flaming variety). With no street lighting whatsoever, you'll be relying on the moon and stars when darkness falls.

TRAVEL WARNING

Some parts of the country – the rockier highland routes in particular – are infested with bandits. If you plan to travel overland, try to band together with locals going the same way. The frequent wars between states make travel dangerous too.

Plan your route carefully before you set out, or you'll have to take long detours to avoid troublespots. Sparta in particular is usually at war and you don't want to get caught up in a battle, or worse, arrested as a spy.

Bandits lie in wait for the footsore and travel-worn.

SEA TRAVEL

Wherever possible, make journeys by sea. Boats are the easiest and quickest way to travel and you're sure to find a merchant ship to take you – for a reasonable fee. Greece has hundreds of natural inlets and creeks, which means wherever you are you're close to the sea. Even heading inland, you can probably make most of the trip by boat.

The best time to sail is summer, though remember boats rely on windpower. Ironically, you'll face delays if the weather's too good and your ship is becalmed. There's also the threat of

An early anchor

storms, the rocky coast and, worse still, pirates. Luckily, your visit coincides with a time when the Athenian navy is most powerful. With the seas carefully policed, pirate ships are at an all time low.

But be warned: pirates don't all sail under the Jolly Roger. It's not unknown for a crew to turn on their own passengers and rob them once they're out at sea. So, be careful whose ship you board. And make sure the captain offers a sacrifice to the sea god Poseidon before you set out. It can't hurt and shows he takes his responsibility seriously.

TOP TIPS FOR TOURISTS

No. 5: Travel inn

As you've probably already found, inns are few and far between. Luckily for the tourist, the Ancient Greeks have a custom of hospitality. In fact, it's more of a duty. If you need a place to stay, you can knock on almost any door and be sure of a welcome. But treat your hosts with respect and be sure to repay them handsomely, with gifts from home.

❝ ...in order to defraud their creditors, they laid a plot to sink [the ship] ❞

Demosthenes, a great orator
(with a useful reminder to be careful whose ship you travel on)

A merchant ship to avoid: its crew looks distinctly unfriendly

There are stories of hapless passengers being thrown overboard and rescued by dolphins – but you can't rely on them.

IF YOU GET SICK...

You've come to the right place. Greek doctors have excellent reputations. They tend to fall into two camps – though these aren't mutually exclusive. Some, mainly priests, believe in the old ideas, swearing by Asclepius, the god of healing. But many others now follow Hippocrates, man of medicine.

PRIESTS & PRAYERS

Most families rely on herbal cures. If these fail, they call in a priest. In fact, sleeping in one of Asclepius' temples has been known to produce miraculous results. If not, the priests can offer home-made remedies of their own.

Visit a temple and you'll have to perform certain sacrifices before spending the night. You must also undergo a "purification" ceremony, probably involving vast amounts of holy water. Ideally, Asclepius should heal you as you sleep. Or, he may tell you via a dream the treatment you need. Of course, you may also wake up no better.

A THANK-YOU GIFT

If Asclepius does help, you should leave him an offering – usually a model of the body part he's cured. That may be fine if you had a sore foot. For a more embarrassing problem, you may prefer to forget priests and try a scientific approach.

THE NEW SCIENCE

For the latest thinking, consult a doctor who follows the Hippocratic method. Hippocrates has founded a medical school on his home island of Kos. Try to find a doctor who trained there. Having learned the basics of diagnosis, he'll ask questions and examine you to try to discover what's wrong. He'll have had anatomy lessons too – probably on live subjects – so he has some idea of what's going on under your skin.

Wow!!

An anatomy lesson

Don't think the new doctors will knock Asclepius, though. Praying still has its place. They're simply more practical, following the radical line that illness isn't a punishment from the gods, but has natural causes. More shocking to local patients is the theory that doctors can cure them without divine help.

Dreaming a cure

14

Blood letting – if you let them.

THE CURE

Your prescription will include herbal medicine and lots of rest. Like Hippocrates, many doctors believe that most ailments clear up on their own. But, like the priests, they also call for sacrifices – in the form of a healthy diet and more exercise. The doctor may be after your blood too. Literally. Even in these enlightened times, blood is believed to carry disease. If the doctor offers to open a vein, make your excuses and leave.

HEALTH INSURANCE

Don't worry, you won't need it. If you bring enough spices to barter with, you can be sure of the doctor of your choice. Even if you don't have a bean (or, more usefully, a peppercorn), you'll still be able to get medical treatment. Under the Greek equivalent of a modern public health system, the state funds doctors so the poor can be treated free of charge.

66 ...it arises from natural causes; men think it divine because they do not understand it. 99

Herodotus, a historian
(He was talking about epilepsy, known as the "Sacred Disease".)

Surgical instruments

Bone drill

Hooks

Bone forceps

Uvula forceps

Scalpels

Knives

TOP TIPS FOR TOURISTS

No. 6: Under the knife

If you think you'll need an operation, head home. Though surgery is performed, it's all done without the aid of drugs, either to kill germs or – more significantly – your pain. Even for the Ancient Greeks, operations are a last resort. Those patients who don't die of shock on the table, usually die of infection soon after. If that doesn't put you off, just look at the instruments on the right.

TALK THE TALK

Ancient Greece is a nation of talkers and discussion is almost the national pastime. The prime example of this is the *symposium*: far-reaching debates, on any topic you can think of, which follows dessert at a dinner party.

Male guests often bring along female companions, called *hetairai*, to amuse them. No invitation is needed, but they must be bright, pretty, young and witty. Female time tourists should grab the chance for a girls' night in.

Painting of a hetaira

TOP TIPS FOR TOURISTS

No. 7: ☞ Riddle-me-ree

One of the most popular after-dinner games is asking riddles, with forfeits (such as drinking a glass of salty wine), if you get the answer wrong. A couple are given below, to let you know what you're in for. (The answers are upside down at the bottom of page 17.)

(1) *Don't speak and you'll express my name; say my name and you won't express me at all!*

(2) *Look at me and I'll look back, but I won't see you: I have no eyes. If you talk, my lips will move, but without a sound: I have no voice.*

COTTEBOS ☞

For modern males, the *symposium* might not sound like that much fun anyway. But don't worry – it isn't all talk. You'll be entertained with music, dancing, acrobatics and the much-loved game, *cottebos*.

If you play a sport which involves throwing objects at a target, you'll have a head start. The steps to the game are shown below. Try to get it right first time, because the worse you are, the more you'll drink.

1. Don't finish your drink to the very last mouthful.

2. Instead, swirl the dregs around the bowl.

3. Hurl the contents at a target.

4. Miss and get your bowl refilled.

16

Tokens with a solid middle mean "innocent".

A PHILOSOPHY MATCH

Philosophy comes from the Greek word for "lover of knowledge". The earliest philosophers studied everything. But, in recent times, the study has been refined to consider the purpose of the universe and the meaning of life. If you want to hear the moral and philosophical questions of the day being discussed, head for any market place. Philosophers gather crowds of students around them – too big a gathering for any house – so they meet in the open air.

Tokens with a hollow middle mean "guilty".

GUILTY!

Female tourists, fed up at being left out of the *symposium*, could watch a trial. Remember, though, only citizens vote on the verdict. With no lawyers, citizens conduct their own cases. Some even hire writers (don't worry, all speeches are timed). The outcome is decided by an odd number of men, to prevent a 50:50 split, and there are several hundred on the jury. (A dozen would be too easy to bribe.)

A SPOTTER'S GUIDE TO PHILOSOPHERS

Socrates: the father of philosophy, you may only know of Socrates as a bald old man with a long beard. At the time of your visit, he's about 35. Grab the chance to see him in action before his fame spreads. Just look for the ugly philosopher discussing truth, good and evil.

Socrates

Plato: a pupil of Socrates, who will write down his teacher's ideas and develop his own on the ideal way to run a state.

Plato

Aristotle: a pupil of Plato (born after your visit) with a broad knowledge of politics and science.

Aristotle

Stoics: named after the *stoa* (porch) where they meet. Pass by and you'll hear them extol the benefits of living a calm life.

Diogenes: founder of the group known as *Cynics*, who don't believe in rules and dislike too much wealth. At least Diogenes lives his beliefs. He's recently moved into a large jar.

Diogenes

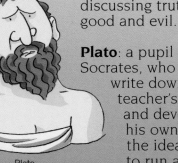

17

TEMPLES

On a trip here, you don't just visit the houses of famous people: you can tour the homes of gods. The Greeks believe the gods are just like humans, only more so. They even share the same needs, including having somewhere to live. Other churches may be places to worship. Greek temples are the godly version of luxury apartments (though without the kitchen or bathroom). In fact, most people pray at home, mainly heading to the temples to celebrate festivals and holidays.

BIGGER AND BETTER

Early temples weren't that luxurious as homes go. At first, a god was lucky if he got more than one room. As time went on, designers became more ambitious.

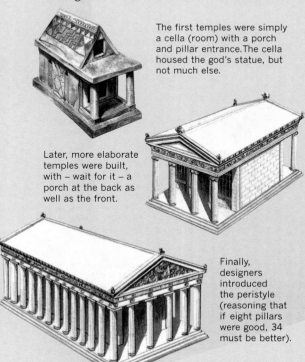

The first temples were simply a cella (room) with a porch and pillar entrance. The cella housed the god's statue, but not much else.

Later, more elaborate temples were built, with – wait for it – a porch at the back as well as the front.

Finally, designers introduced the peristyle (reasoning that if eight pillars were good, 34 must be better).

RITES & WRONGS

While visiting a temple, you may want to enter into the spirit of the thing and pray to a god.* Take a present. It needn't be flashy, but find out which gifts your god likes. (Most gods are notoriously fussy.)

Leaving a charred offering outside a temple

Luckily, priests are usually on hand to advise you and you'll find them very approachable. Around here, they're like teachers or doctors: being a priest is just a job. At work, they may be holy; at home, they're like everyone else.

TOP TIPS FOR TOURISTS

No. 8: Let us pray

Calling upon a god isn't simply a case of kneeling down, with hands together. You address most gods with your arms high above your head, hands to the sky. (Unless you're trying to catch the attention of an Underworld god, when your palms should face the ground.) If you're addressing a sky god, face East; for a marine god, face the sea. It's largely a matter of common sense. (And if your prayers are ignored, try turning around.)

* There are plenty to choose: see pages 50-2.

THE PARTHENON

With the Classical Period, temple design is in its heyday. And the best example is the **Parthenon**, built between 447 and 438BC. If you see only one temple, make it this one. Dedicated to *Athene Parthenos*, patron goddess of Athens, the Parthenon sits high above the city. Of all the temples on the Acropolis, this is the star attraction and well worth the climb.

> *Zeus, give us what is good for us, whether we have asked for it or not, and keep us far from evil, even if we should ask for it.*

A prayer by Socrates

In her right hand Athene holds a statuette of Nike, goddess of victory. Her left rests on a shield supported by a serpent.

Before you stagger in, catch your breath by looking at the incredible marble sculptures decorating the outside of the temple. They're the work of Pheidias, one of the great artists of the day. Come shortly after 438BC and they'll still be new enough for you to see the paint dry. Inside, one sight stands head and shoulders above the rest – and you: the statue of *Athene Parthenos*.

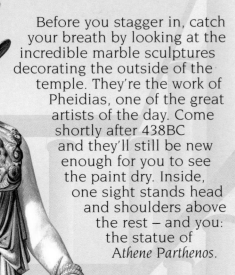

The statue of Athene, inside the Parthenon

The statue is said to have cost more than the entire temple – up close, you can see why.

Though the figure is made of wood and ivory, her dress is made of beaten gold.

The statue stands 12m (40ft) high. You might want to take binoculars to see her face (just don't get spotted).

FESTIVALS

Whatever time of year you visit, your trip is bound to coincide with a festival. With no weekends off, festivals are the only breaks the Greeks get. Basically parties for the gods enjoyed by humans, festivals offer music, drama, sports and plenty of food. (It's easy to forget their main goal is persuading gods to grant prayers.)

The procession of Panathenea

TWO GODS AND A TREE

Most festivals finish up at the temples on the **Acropolis**. At the site of what will be the Erectheion Temple, you'll be standing on the spot of a legendary contest. For it's here, so the story goes, that Poseidon and Athene fought over who should be the city's patron.

Poseidon promised the city vast wealth through a spring of sea water. Athene simply planted an olive tree. The Greeks obviously thought the tree of more immediate value, because Athene was declared the winner and Athens was born. You can still see her tree growing in the courtyard, one of the city's most sacred spots.

A new dress of gold is carried by boat to Athene's statue on the Acropolis.

Dancers, musicians, soldiers and priests all process along the Panathenaic Way.

BEST OF THE FESTS

If you're in Athens over the summer, look out for the *Panathenea*, held each year for Athene. Every four years it becomes the Great Panathenea and lasts for six days. It's a great chance to dress up: even Athene gets a new frock. Music and dancing are followed by sports, with olive oil as prizes. Highlight of the festival is a procession to the Acropolis.

Important citizens lead the parade, followed by the offering bearers.

The Panathenea procession leaves from the Dipylon Gate: just follow the crowds.

One hundred cows are led to the Acropolis where they're sacrificed.

THE PICK OF THE REST

Come in February and you'll be here for the *Antihesteria*. Wine from the previous year's harvest is sold and a statue of Dionysus is carried through the streets to his temple. On the last day, banquets are prepared for the spirits of the dead and placed on household altars.

In a festival similar to "Trick or Treating", children go from door to door for fruit and cakes. (But there are no tricks and the closest they get to dressing up is carrying poles wound with wool.) If you fancy a night-time festival, celebrate *Hephestia*. Held for *Hephaestus* (blacksmith of the gods), in November, teams of runners compete by torchlight.

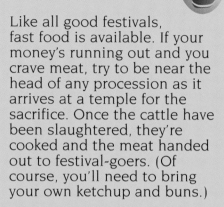

TOP TIPS FOR TOURISTS

No. 9: Hungry for hamburgers?

Like all good festivals, fast food is available. If your money's running out and you crave meat, try to be near the head of any procession as it arrives at a temple for the sacrifice. Once the cattle have been slaughtered, they're cooked and the meat handed out to festival-goers. (Of course, you'll need to bring your own ketchup and buns.)

❝ *When I was seven I carried the sacred symbols... when I was grown up handsome I carried the sacred basket...* ❞

Chorus of women from the play "Lysistrata" by Aristophanes

FESTIVAL CALENDAR

Month		Festival	God/goddess*
Skirophorion	June/July	Arrephoroi	Athene
		Dipoleia	Zeus
		Diisoteria	Zeus & Athene
Hekatombion	July/August	Panathenea	Athene
Roedromion	September/October	Mysteries	Demeter
Pyanopsion	October/November	Chalkeia (Feast of the smiths)	Athene & Hephaestus
Maimakterion	November/December	Maimakteria	Zeus
Antihesteria	February/March	Lenaia	Dionysus
		Diasia	Zeus/Meilichios
Elaphebolion	March/April	Great Dionysia	Dionysus
Thargelion	May/June	Thargelia	Apollo & Artemis

* For more on the gods, see pages 50-52.

THE PLAY'S THE THING

The most serious Greek plays are tragedies. With their grand themes (murder, conflict, blood all over the dinner table), they could easily turn into gore-fests. Don't worry if you're squeamish. Violence takes place in the wings with a narrator telling you what's happening. The odd "dead" body may be carted on stage, but that's as gruesome as it gets.

An actor "corpsing"

LIGHT RELIEF

If doom and gloom are not for you, try comedies, or "satyr" plays. Comedies, as the name implies, are the opposite of tragedies and focus on lighter concerns. Much of the fun, however, is at the expense of the stars and politics of the day (not unlike pantomimes). To get every joke, you'll probably have to bone up on current affairs first. "Satyr" plays are comedies which poke fun at tragedies. The name comes from some of the cast who dress as satyrs: half-men, half-beasts.

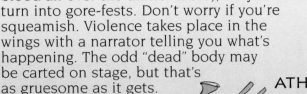

A buffoon in a comedy

A satyr acting in a tragi-comedy or a comi-tragedy.

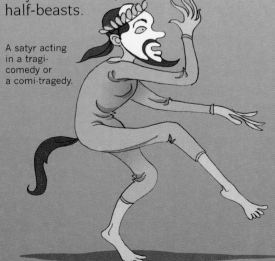

ATHENS DRAMA FESTIVAL

Drama addicts should visit Athens during the *Dionysia*. Named after Dionysus (the god of wine), it's a combined religious and drama fest and lasts for five days. After the first day's processions and sacrifices come the drama competitions. Each year, three tragedy and five comedy playwrights make the shortlist. You may see the première of a play which will still be being performed in 2,500 years' time.

BIRTH OF THE PLAY

The *Dionysia* began as an ancient countryside festival. A group of singers and dancers, called the "chorus" and all wearing masks, enacted various legends. There could be up to 50 of them, reciting in unison. Every so often, one actor would have a solo. Gradually, the chorus grew smaller and three actors became full-time soloists, sharing up to 45 parts. Now, the dialogue between soloists is the most important part. The chorus stays in the background, passing the odd comment and linking events.

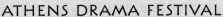

A tragic actor

THE "MODERN" STAGE

At first, plays were put on in the marketplace. The audience sat in wooden stands put up for the festival each year. But one year the stands collapsed, killing several of the audience, so a permanent, open-air arena was built of stone. Drama is now so popular, similar arenas can be found in every major city in the Greek world.

An open-air arena

The actors change in here.

Altar

Chorus members sing and dance in the *orchestra* (dancing floor).

Male and female parts are played by men.

The arenas can hold up to 18,000 spectators.

SETTING THE SCENE

In such vast arenas, from a distance the actors look little more than performing fleas. So, the costumes are designed to let you know who they're playing. Happy characters are dressed brightly. Tragic ones wear dark clothes. The costumes are often heavily padded and actors wear platform boots and huge wigs to help them stand out.

Actors wear painted masks made of stiffened fabric or cork, so you can see their expressions from a distance. The large mouths amplify the actors' voices.

TOP TIPS FOR TOURISTS

No. 10: Box office

Instead of tickets, you'll need tokens. These have a letter showing which row your seat is in. Blocks of seats are divided into city districts, so if you want to sit with friends from another part of town, buy your tickets together. They cost two *obols** each. You should also check when you book if females in your party may sit with you. And don't worry if you're stuck at the back. The arenas have fantastic acoustics. Wherever you sit, you'll hear every word.

*One *obol* = 1/6 *drachma*; tickets cost about a third of an average day's pay

ENTERTAINMENT

Greek drama isn't to everyone's taste, but there are plenty of other pastimes and diversions, from the high-brow music, poetry and dance to the low-brow board games and games of chance.

The youngest tourists aren't left out either. Toddling siblings can be amused with numerous wooden toys, including dolls, hoops, rattles and tops. And if you're a whizz with yoyos back home, here's your chance to shine. Children here have yoyos too, though not flashing plastic ones.

Shakers

Hand-held drum called a timpanon

Cymbals

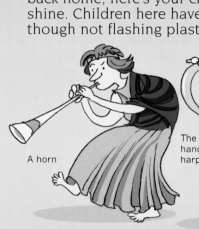

A horn

The lyre, a hand-held harp

Pipes called auloi

Getting into the party spirit

Panpipes

MUSIC & MOVEMENT

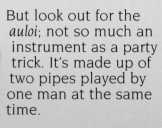

You're in for a surprise where Greek music is concerned: no one in modern times has ever heard any. Because there's no written music from the period, it's impossible to recreate in the 21st century. The instruments should be largely familiar, even if the sound they make together isn't. The harp, cymbals and panpipes are all around in a similar form today.

But look out for the *auloi*; not so much an instrument as a party trick. It's made up of two pipes played by one man at the same time.

You may be tempted to dance to the music, but don't try any modern routines. People here consider dancing one of the highest art forms and expect it to be always both beautiful and expressive.

RAPPING RHAPSODES

For the tone-deaf there is always literature, though even here, poetry has a musical slant. It truly is performance art, usually read aloud but often sung or chanted with a musical backing. Think of it as the forerunner of rapping. In fact the men who earn their living by reciting poetry at religious festivals are called *rhapsodes*.

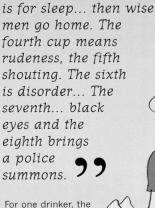

Painting of a rhapsode

If you'd like to pick up extra cash by busking this way, you'll need a good memory. *Rhapsodes* know the epic poems (one of which fills several books) by heart. If they ask for requests, suggest *The Iliad* or *The Odyssey*. These two epics of Greek history were written 400 years ago by the poet Homer.

GAMES

If the above is too cultural for you, there are less intellectual pursuits. One very popular game is "Blind Man's Buff" (think "Tag" with a blindfold), enjoyed by adults and children alike. For the energetic, there's a ball game similar to hockey. But if you prefer your fun sitting down, try dice or knuckle bones.

JUST THE ONE...

One activity everyone enjoys is a drink or two of (watered down) wine. Before you're tempted to follow suit, you might like to read the words of warning in the quote below. It's a saying currently doing the rounds in Athens.

" *The first cup means health, the second pleasure. The third cup is for sleep... then wise men go home. The fourth cup means rudeness, the fifth shouting. The sixth is disorder... The seventh... black eyes and the eighth brings a police summons.* "

For one drinker, the party is definitely over...

TOP TIPS FOR TOURISTS

No. 11: Amuse a Muse

Crucial to any artist, whether writer, dancer or musician, is inspiration. The Ancient Greeks believe this comes from nine goddesses called Muses, each responsible for a separate art form. If your verses don't scan, your pipe sounds like a hoarse duck, or you dance with two left feet, try calling on one of them for help.

ART & SCULPTURE

Even if you have little interest in museums, you can't avoid Greek art. Sculptures are everywhere: in homes and temples, even the street. Early statues copied the Egyptian style and were admittedly stiff stuff. But in recent years art has undergone a makeover, and some of the work being produced is amazing.

An Egyptian sculpture: a pharaoh in formal (and clunky) pose

The Greek version: so lifelike you'd think the statue was about to throw its discus

THE NEW PERFECTIONISM

Classical sculptors are perfecting the knack of showing the human body, caught in a moment in time. Statues are noted for their beauty and serenity; even those in athletic poses have a flowing grace. As for the clothes draped around the bodies: you may have to touch them to prove they're made of stone not fabric.

This famous boxer was actually made later than your trip. But it's a good example of the more realistic direction sculptures will take.

TOP TIPS FOR TOURISTS
No. 12: What a relief

A life-sized marble statue may be impractical to cart home. But if you're hooked on Greek art, don't worry. Mini versions of temple carvings are made as offerings. You could commission one for your wall. Small terracotta figures in scenes from daily life are also popular – and would easily fit in a backpack.

SELF-EXPRESSION

Greek artists are especially adept at portraying human emotions and eager to show off by sculpting stars of the day. They do a fine line in beautiful goddesses, too. Pheidias is the name on everyone's lips. Apart from his statue of Athene on the Acropolis, he made the incredible one of Zeus at Olympia.

PRODUCTION LINE

Statues are carved from marble or limestone, or shaped from bronze. The stone ones are cut roughly into shape as they're quarried, to make them easier to transport to the workshops. If you're quiet, a sculptor may let you watch him at work.

Once carved, marble statues are painted to create a lifelike appearance. Glass or stones are used for eyes and statues are even accessorized, with crowns, weapons and jewels, all made from bronze.

Seeing a flowing figure appear from a lump of stone (if you can wait around for two months) is almost a supernatural experience.

A sculptor's workshop

FACTORY FINISH

Athenian sculptors have a growing reputation. As their fame spreads, demand for the statues has been outstripping supply. Factories are now springing up at quarries, so sculptures can be produced on-site and exported all over the Mediterranean.

Carving out a scene of gods to be built into a temple

A RELIEF FROM STATUES

Statues aren't the only expression of Greek art. Sculptors also carve slabs of stone with "reliefs": scenes with figures which stand out against a flat background. They're mostly found on temples (check out the Parthenon for some fantastic examples). To take a more unusual art tour, visit the local graveyard. Athens, especially, is known for its spectacular gravestones.

27

ARCHITECTURE & BUILDINGS

Greek architecture will make an impression on everyone over the years, from the Romans (who'll copy everything they can get their hands on), to Renaissance Italians, modern designers and architects.

The architecture is all based on mathematics. The proportions of Ancient Greek buildings, the height and width of columns, for example, are carefully calculated. It's this that gives the buildings their air of well-balanced elegance. In layman's terms: they look good.

BACK TO BASICS

All public buildings (private homes aren't so important) follow the same basic design. A series of vertical columns is topped with a horizontal beam (the *lintel*). This is said to be a development from much earlier buildings, where tree trunks were used to support the roofs.

The Doric style is a simple design, with broad, plain columns.

The Ionic is more elegant and decorative than Doric. Columns are slender and their tops ("capitals" to use the technical term), are decorated.

There are some variations, though. The different styles are called "orders" and there are two main ones to look out for: *Doric* and *Ionic*. As you sightsee, see how many of each you can spot. You get extra points if you find *Corinthian* or *Aeolic* columns (both a form of the Ionic). They're not used all that often.

TOP TIPS FOR TOURISTS

No. 13: Casing the joint?

Be careful not to hang around the back of a temple. It's where the treasury is located. The guards may not believe your excuse that you're just an architecture fan – and Athenian jails are not places you'd want to visit.

Corinthian column

Aeolic column

BUILDING WORKS

All cities are usually undergoing some major construction and the Greek city-states are no exception. The only things missing from the ancient skyline are cranes. Public buildings are continually being commissioned and a Greek building site is an eye-opening experience.

Most buildings are constructed from marble or limestone, with wooden beams supporting the roof. Roofs have terracotta or, more rarely, marble tiles and the outsides of buildings are decorated with painted statues and sculpted reliefs.

Since Pericles is having all of the temples on the Acropolis rebuilt, you'll have the chance to see at least one being put up. Stop for a while and watch the builders at work. They do an impressive job of putting up these vast structures with neither cranes nor cement.

A temple building site

Blocks are joined together with metal rods called dowels, which fit through the middle of each block.

Stones are carved with mallet and chisel and hoisted into place using ropes and pulleys.

BATTLE OF THE BULGE

When you're standing by a temple, its columns towering over you, take a closer look. Seen from below, a column with completely straight sides appears thinner in the middle. To combat this, architects have designed a bulge into their columns. They then go in at the top, drawing your eye up to the magnificent carvings around the roof.

Columns with and without a bulge

29

ARCADES & AGORAS

Shopping: love it or hate it, in Ancient Greece you can't avoid it. The agora, or marketplace, is at the heart of every Greek city. It's not a bad place to start your sightseeing in each new town. You can stock up on any supplies that are running low at the same time. It's also where to change your coins into the local currency.

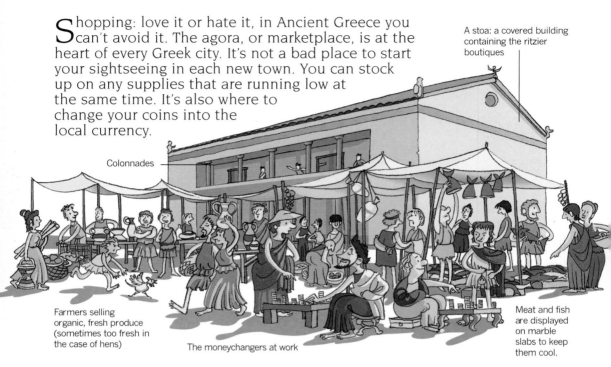

A stoa: a covered building containing the ritzier boutiques

Colonnades

Farmers selling organic, fresh produce (sometimes too fresh in the case of hens)

The moneychangers at work

Meat and fish are displayed on marble slabs to keep them cool.

CHANGING MONEY

Before you can shop, you'll need a moneychanger. Look for the wealthy men behind tables (and piles of money). If your Greek is up to it, you could just ask for the *trapezitai* (which means "table men"). They'll change coins from all of the city-states, although – like *bureaux de change* everywhere – they charge commission. And check your coins closely. Worn coins which are too light are rejected by traders.

It's worth noting that the *trapezitai* also act as bankers. Deposit some change with them and you won't have to lug heavy purse-loads of coins around with you.

SHOPPING ARCADES

If you prefer upmarket shopping to an open market, head for the covered buildings called *stoae*. Stores lined up behind rows of colonnades (columns), offer everything from pricey jewels to lamps. You can also pick up offerings, such as incense or honeycakes, for any temples you may plan to visit. But you can't browse; you'll have to squint. Most shops are simply open rooms with a counter where the front wall should be.

UNDER THE COLONNADES

The shady colonnades are an ideal place to meet friends. You could buy a snack in the market, but remember: only the lower classes and slaves eat in public.

THE PRODUCE POLICE

You may have been to markets whose stall holders weren't all above board. Traders in the *agora* are monitored by various officials. In Athens, ten *metronomoi* are also chosen each year to check the accuracy of traders' weights and measures. And if you're unhappy with the quality of an item you've bought, complain to the *agoranomoi*: the Greeks' trading standards officers.

An Athenian coin

SLAVES FOR SALE

One "product" you might prefer not to see on sale is people. But, as in many of the ancient civilizations, slavery is a fact of life. Not even Greek citizens are immune. If they're captured as prisoners of war, they can be sold on as slaves to citizens in another city-state.

Slave auction on a podium

A successful bidder

TOP TIPS FOR TOURISTS

No. 14: Retail therapy for men

Back home, men may leave the shopping to women. They don't get away with that here. Men do almost all of it (and that includes buying food). Female tourists may be more astonished to learn that they won't be allowed to buy things over a certain amount. If an expensive souvenir takes your fancy, you will have to persuade a male companion to buy it for you.

WORKSHOPS & CRAFTSMEN

Close to the agora you'll find local craftsmen. They often set up shop (and home) nearby, to encourage customers to visit. If you want something made, such as a pair of shoes (and you'll be around to collect them), this is where to place your order. Craftsmen often cluster together, with all the potters in one area, for example. It certainly makes life easier when comparing prices and styles.

POT MANIA

Ancient Greek pots are exported all over the known world. You might think about buying some: they'll become collector's items. The first pots made after the Dark Ages were simply decorated with geometric patterns (and, later, human and animal figures). But, about 200 years ago, contact with the wider world led to a craze for Egyptian designs.

These days, pots show scenes from myths and daily life. Take a pot instead of a photo for a snapshot of Greek life to show friends at home. (Even if you brought a camera, using it might lead to awkward questions.) Early examples have black figures on a red background.

RED IS THE NEW BLACK

The latest fashion is for "red-figure ware". The clay used turns red when fired. Red-figure pots are painted black with spaces left for the figures. When the pots come out of the kiln, the painted areas have stayed black but the blank figure shapes have turned red. Finer details are then added with white or dark red paint.

Two examples of red-figure ware

POTS FOR EVERY OCCASION: A SHOPPER'S GUIDE

Aryballos
Flask for perfumed oils

Alabastron
Flask for perfumed oils and ointments

Loutrophoros
Ceremonial vase to carry water for a bridal bath

Pyxis
Medicine box

Amphora*
Storage jar for oil or wine

Hydria*
Water carrier

Kylix
Drinking cup

Skyphos
Drinking cup

Kantharos
Drinking cup

Calyx Krater*
For turning water into wine...

Volute Krater*
Krater with spiral handles

Oinochoe
Serving jug

* If you want one of these, take a friend. They're too big for one person to carry.

SOUVENIR GUIDE

There's nothing worse when you're away (apart from the unavoidable tourist tummy), than traipsing around looking for things to take home as gifts. That huge *krater*, such a familiar sight at meal times, may well look out of place in your mother's kitchen. And trendy as your dad likes to think he is, he can hardly go to a football game in a tunic.

Your best bet is to go for light, easily portable items. (It may sound obvious but look at all the tourists struggling home through customs and you'll see it needs repeating.)

Ideal choices are statuettes or small pieces of pottery. If you do go for a statuette, avoid the junk specifically designed for the tourist market.

Impulse purchases are never a good idea.

Other gifts you could consider include high-quality embroidered robes, rings and brooches, and cosmetics. If you're really stuck, there's always olive oil. But pack it carefully or you'll end up with soggy, greasy clothes and no gift.

> 66 *You will find everything sold together in the same place at Athens.* 99
>
> **Euboulos, a poet**

TOP TIPS FOR TOURISTS

No. 15: Sparing Granny's blushes

Most Greeks have a remarkably relaxed attitude to the human body. This is perhaps inevitable in a place so hot you wear as little as possible. It does mean, however, that they are quite happy to plaster all sorts of dubious images over their pottery.

Many vases have very explicit scenes (red-figure ware in particular), so choose souvenirs for your grandparents carefully. Unless you have broad-minded elderly relatives, it might be safer to bring them back olives.

A risqué wine cooler

CENSORED

33

PIRAEUS, PORT OF ATHENS

Just 9 kms (5½ miles) southwest of Athens lies the city's port, **Piraeus**. All of the imports and most visitors entering the city arrive here first. If you've spent a few quiet days on a beach, go to Piraeus for excitement. The place buzzes with activity. You can mingle with merchants, share a drink with a sailor or bask in the sun watching ship builders at work.

You'll see people from every nation, and fellow tourists from Phoenicia, Egypt, Persia and Babylon. Don't be surprised if the locals call them "barbarians", despite their often elegant and cultured appearance.

"Barbarian" is the name given to all foreigners, because, to the Greeks, they seem to say "baa-baa".

A WALL WALK

Set out for Piraeus from Athens and you'll follow one of the major sights, the **Long Walls** (*Makra Teiche*). Work began on them in 460BC to link the city to the port, thanks to Pericles. He saw the disaster waiting to happen if an enemy cut off Athens from its navy and port, the main source of supplies.

66 *From all the lands, everything enters.* 99

Thucydides (a politician and historian) describing Piraeus

A scene from the docks at Piraeus

Tasting the produce

Traders

TOP TIPS FOR TOURISTS

No. 16: Bird's eye view

For the best overview of the walls and a chance to see all the way back to Athens, climb **Munychia Hill**. Topped by a temple to Athene Munychia, it offers the best view in the area.

SNACKS & SOUVENIRS

Piraeus is where to find last-minute mementos, plus lunch to sustain what could be a mammoth shop. For really extravagant buys, such as silk, head to a warehouse on the docks. Shipments are stored here before being sent around the country. Look for items which didn't survive the sea journey that well. You may pick up a bargain. To see the range of imports and where they come from (and to write a shopping list), check the map:

BRIEF HISTORY OF PIRAEUS

Piraeus, with its three natural ports and closeness to Athens, is one of the city's biggest assets. But this wasn't realized and exploited until 493BC. Themistocles, a ruler of Athens, had a wall built around the city and turned it into a naval headquarters. Piraeus has been redesigned recently, to make better use of the three ports, Karanthos, Munychia and Zea.

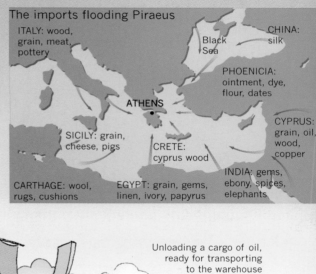

The imports flooding Piraeus

ITALY: wood, grain, meat, pottery

CHINA: silk

Black Sea

PHOENICIA: ointment, dye, flour, dates

ATHENS

CYPRUS: grain, oil, wood, copper

SICILY: grain, cheese, pigs

CRETE: cyprus wood

INDIA: gems, ebony, spices, elephants

CARTHAGE: wool, rugs, cushions

EGYPT: grain, gems, linen, ivory, papyrus

Unloading a cargo of oil, ready for transporting to the warehouse

Catch of the day: fish is plentiful and very fresh

Cooking lunch for the sailors, dockhands and tourists

THE OLYMPIC GAMES

The original Olympic Games began way back in 776BC and are part of the Pan-Hellenic games, the sports fixture of the year. Held at **Olympia** every four years, they last five days, the focus of a festival to celebrate the god Zeus. Heralds travel to every Greek state announcing the date and warring states call a three-month truce so you, and every other tourist, can travel to Olympia safely.

SPECTATOR SPORT FOR MEN

When you arrive, pitch your tent at the camp by the river, then wander around to take in the atmosphere. Masses of things are provided for the celebrities and visitors who descend during the Games. Souvenir stalls line the roads by the stadium. There are sightseeing tours, shrines to visit, even poetry recitals. You could also try using the – Olympic-sized – pool (when the athletes aren't in it).

Don't forget the religious side of things. Pilgrims worship at Zeus' temple, worth visiting for the ivory and gold statue of Zeus, standing 13m (43ft) high. It's a good idea to take a gift – it need only be incense or wine. But set out early. People start lining up to get in at dawn.

The Olympic village

Training area for jumping and wrestling

The Gymnasium: a training ground for running and throwing events

Temple of Zeus

The stadium

YOUR GUIDE TO EVENTS

WARNING! These athletes are clothed. In real life, they wear nothing but a layer of oil (to protect against sunburn).

Running: the oldest event, the stadium track is 192m (640ft) long; made of clay covered with sand. There are three races: *stade* (1 length); *diaulos* (2 lengths) and *dolichos* (20 or 24 lengths).

Wrestling: fans get to see three types: **upright**, where an opponent must be thrown to the ground three times; **ground**, where one fighter must simply give in; and **pankration**, the most dangerous, a mix of wrestling and boxing. Only two tactics are banned: biting and eye-gouging.

Pentathlon: made up of five events – running, wrestling, jumping, discus and javelin throwing – the goal is to find the best all-rounder.

Boxing: you'll need almost as much stamina as the fighters, as boxing matches can last for hours. They're only decided when one fighter loses consciousness or concedes defeat – so most blows are aimed at the head and virtually any blow with the hand is OK.

Chariot & horse racing: chariot drivers race 12 laps around two posts in the ground. Jockeys ride bareback over 1.2km (¾ mile). Both can be nasty as accidents are common.

Arena for chariot and horse races

INSIDE THE STADIUM

Judges watch events from seats in a special stand in the stadium. You'll simply stand. But the stadium holds 40,000, so you should get in.

You get an excellent view of the Games from the grassy slopes surrounding the stadium.

Track events in the stadium open the first day. A trumpet blasts, the judges take their seats, then more trumpets are followed by a herald announcing the first race. Only citizens and non-criminals can take part, so the herald then calls out the names of competitors. After each event, a herald gives the name of the winner, his father's name and his city.

Statue of a female Greek runner

GAMES FOR WOMEN

Only men may compete in the Games. Married women can't even watch, on pain of death. Single women aren't exactly welcome, either. Instead, they have their own festival, *Heraia*, for the goddess Hera. Also held every four years, it has running races for girls of various ages.

WINNING SPONSORSHIP

Prizes are given on the last day of the Games and include ribbons, olive wreaths and palm branches. Athletes are meant to seek only the glory of competing and winning, but many become professionals. Cities gain prestige from sponsoring successful athletes, so they put up statues of them and make them payments on the quiet.

Grateful city officials and a winning athlete

TOP TIPS FOR TOURISTS

No. 17: The judges' decision is final

Though there are many rules and regulations for competitors, as a spectator you need only remember one. Never disagree with the judges in public. Cries of, "Oh come off it, ref! Are you blind?" may be OK at home. At the Games, you risk a fine – or worse.

37

ORACLES & OTHER MYSTERIES

Unsure what to do next? Visit an oracle! It's a good introduction to an important part of Greek life and you may get some hints on planning the rest of your stay. Oracles are the Greek way of seeking advice from the gods. Rather confusingly, when a local refers to an oracle, he could mean one of three things: a priestess speaking for a god; the sacred place where she speaks; or the message itself. Whichever it is, oracles are consulted for all major decisions, and some minor ones.

THE ORACLE AT DELPHI

The most famous — and the one to visit — is the oracle at **Delphi**. It's about 160km (100 miles) from Athens, built around a sacred spring on the slopes of Mount Parnassus. Here, the god Apollo gives his answers via a priestess called the *Pythia*. Originally, she only gave sittings once a year. But the oracle is now so in demand, hearings take place once a month and two extra "Pythians" have been taken on.

You can ask anything you like and questions range from, "Has my jug been stolen?" to "Should I expand my business?" First, however, Apollo must like you. You'll be asked to make a sacrifice to decide this (and you'll have to pay). Assuming you pass the test, you'll join a line of answer-seekers, drawing lots to see who goes first.

> 66 *Unhappy people, why stay you here? Leave your homes... and flee to the ends of the earth.* 99

Herodotus, *a historian, reporting the Pythia's advice to Athenians in 480BC, just before a Persian attack*

GO-BETWEENS

You can't deal directly with the Pythia. Instead, temple priests will pass on your question and relay the answer. Before you give them the question, make sure you've had a quick dip in the **Castalian Spring**. Like all priests, the Delphic ones are sticklers for cleanliness. You won't be able to see what goes on after you've asked your question, but the picture below should give you some idea.

Inside the inner sanctum

The Pythia sits on a tripod and inhales the smoke of burning laurel leaves.

Then she goes into a trance and gives Apollo's answer. Even the priests don't get to watch — she's hidden behind a curtain.

SOOTHSAYERS

If you're turned down by Apollo, all is not lost. The Greeks don't only look to the gods for answers. Just ask to be directed to the nearest seer or soothsayer: they can see into the future. Not convinced? There are plenty of stories to prove their accuracy, including the legend of Cassandra, a princess of Troy.* She foretold an attack on the city. The Trojans didn't believe a word – until the attack began.

Cassandra was proved right when the Trojans were attacked by Greek soldiers who'd hidden in a giant wooden horse.

THE OMEN

The reliance on the supernatural doesn't stop there. Another option is to consult a "diviner" (reader of signs). Diviners come in three kinds:

1. A seer reads tokens with symbolic signs.

2. An augur reads signs in nature, such as the flight of birds.

3. A haruspex has the gory task of reading the innards of a sacrificed animal.

Of course, you'll have pay for the privilege of their advice. Since the omens can only answer "yes" or "no" you may decide to keep your coin and toss it for an answer. Heads they win, tails you lose...

MYSTERY CULTS

Some citizens join a cult to find the meaning of life. Sadly, the one thing cults have in common is that members are sworn to secrecy. Tourists are definitely <u>not</u> welcome. The closest you'll get is to watch a procession. Each September, members and wannabes of the Eleusinian cult walk from Athens to Eleusis during their initiation ceremony, the "Greater Mysteries"..

TOP TIPS FOR TOURISTS

No. 18: Pythian puzzle

Advice from the Pythia is only the start. She's tricky. Answers are so cleverly phrased, you'd think Apollo was trying to cover all bases. Be warned by the tale of Croesus, a king who asked if he should invade Persia (present-day Iran).

Told he would "destroy a great empire," Croesus attacked and suffered a terrible defeat. When he complained, he was told he had destroyed a great empire: his. (Don't be put off. Plenty of seers hang around the temple to interpret the Pythia's words.)

* An ancient city described in *The Iliad*, a poem by the Greek poet Homer.

39

HOT METAL

If oracles prove just too spiritual, here's the perfect antidote: a trip to the mines at **Laurion**. Sited 65km (40 miles) south of Athens, this is materialism at its best (or worst). Much of the city's wealth comes from the mine with its rich seam of silver-lead. (For those who collect statistics, Laurion is the largest individual supplier of silver to the ancient world.)

The mines are owned by the Athenian state, but leased to private contractors keen to make the quickest buck for the cheapest outlay. Conditions are harsh. Slave-miners work ten-hour shifts and usually die after only three or four years of doing the job.

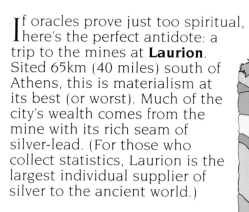

A view of the mine underground (You won't be allowed down.)

The mine is reached via an extremely narrow shaft.

Metal is hauled to the surface in baskets.

Ventilation shaft

Oil lamp

Access is so restricted in some places that miners have to work on their backs.

Up to 20,000 miners work in the mines at any one time.

ABOVE GROUND

You won't be able to see any underground activity, but plenty takes place on the surface. The silver-lead ore leaves the mine with a lot of mine still on it. So, the next stage is washing off the debris, something you may well be able to watch.

Slaves pound the ore with clubs, to break it up from the rock. This is a dusty business and it's a good idea to bring a light scarf to cover your face if you want to watch.

Finally, the crumbly mix is flooded with water and sifted, to rinse the rock dust from the ore.

Breaking up the rock and silver-lead ore

BRONZED OFF

Silver (and gold) are only used for money and precious items. Most everyday Greek objects, and many statues, are made of bronze, a mix of tin and copper. Metalsmiths usually work from home, though in Athens they have their own quarter.

If you want to watch a smith at work, he probably won't mind – but you might like instead to glance at their various ways of working (shown below). Parts of the job are tricky, and ill-timed questions won't be appreciated.

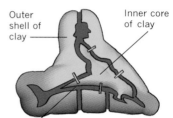

Outer shell of clay —   Inner core of clay

Wax model of a boy on a dolphin between the two layers of clay

1. Hammering method: sheets of bronze are hammered into shape, then riveted together around a wooden core.

2. Casting method: melted bronze is poured into a cast and left to harden.

3. Lost wax method: a wax statue is shaped around a clay core, covered in more clay and heated. The wax melts and is replaced with melted bronze. Once this has set, the outer clay shell is removed.

TOP TIPS FOR TOURISTS

No. 19: Slaves for life

Some slaves in Athens (usually craftsmen), are paid for their work. So, if you're happy with the goods or service provided, you can tip them knowing the money will help buy their freedom. This doesn't happen in Laurion. The mine owners don't want the slaves to have even a chance of leaving. Slip a slave some money and his overseer will pocket it – and probably punish you both.

THE IRON MEN

Iron has only been in use for about 500 years, but it's the preferred metal for weapons and tools, because it's so tough. Iron hasn't replaced bronze entirely though, as it's much more expensive to produce.

Smiths have to heat the iron ore at a very high temperature to extract the metal, which then needs its impurities beaten out.

A furnace for smelting iron

SPARTA: KEEP OUT!

It may seem odd (if not pointless), to read about a city in a guide book which you cannot visit. But if you're wise, reading about Sparta (in some other, safer, city-state), is the closest you'll get.

The Spartans' reputation is such that their name is known in the 21st century: "a spartan room". However bleak the phrase seems, believe us: the real thing is worse. Just reading these pages should convince you that (a) the Spartans are not people to mess with and (b) Sparta is the last place to visit as part of a relaxing vacation.

HARD AS NAILS

The city of Sparta is the strongest military power in Greece. Even though not currently at war, it stays on permanent alert. Every man must join the army, facing a lifetime of training and fighting. But living conditions are basic and uncomfortable for all. Spartans eat plain food and wear the cheapest clothes so there's no risk of their being softened up.

Bronze statue of a Spartan warrior, made in the fifth century BC

TOUGH LOVE

Spartan boys start training for war young.

Boys fight to protect their reputations – and their tunics. (They only get one tunic a year.)

Boys are put in groups and elect a leader to organize them.

A Spartan's hard life begins at birth. In fact, anyone too much of a weakling doesn't get a life. Babies are carefully examined to check their strength. Any not up to scratch are left out to die of exposure. At seven, boys are sent to school where they live in barracks. For the next thirteen years, they're given weapon training, endless athletic fitness sessions and frequent beatings to check their toughness.

WOMEN'S RIGHTS

Spartan women are equally important to the war effort. It's every woman's duty to keep fit to have healthy babies. Unlike the rest of Greece, women here play many sports. They also bring up the children, seeing their husbands (who must live in the army barracks), on rare weekend leave.

FRIENDLY FIRE

Despite their military might, Sparta couldn't withstand a major war alone. So, the Spartans have made various alliances with nearby states in southern Greece. They're known collectively as the Peloponnesian League. These allies have remained independent, but will rush to Sparta's side as and when required.

HELOT OF HARDSHIP

A Spartan soldier, on a rare visit home, overseeing a slave (helot) on his farm

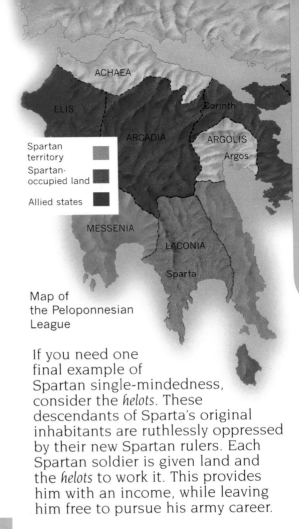

Spartan territory

Spartan-occupied land

Allied states

ACHAEA

ELIS

Corinth

ARCADIA

ARGOLIS

Argos

MESSENIA

LACONIA

Sparta

Map of the Peloponnesian League

If you need one final example of Spartan single-mindedness, consider the *helots*. These descendants of Sparta's original inhabitants are ruthlessly oppressed by their new Spartan rulers. Each Spartan soldier is given land and the *helots* to work it. This provides him with an income, while leaving him free to pursue his army career.

TOP TIPS FOR TOURISTS

No. 20: If you achieve the impossible...

...and do get into Sparta, be warned that on your return to Athens, you won't be greeted with open arms – more likely a spear point. There's currently a state of cold war between the two sides, with Athenians very nervous of Sparta's plans. They are right to be. Things will heat up when war breaks out in 431.

NOT ONE OF US

Only men born in Sparta are citizens. Other men are *perioikoi*: free men who nevertheless have to live in separate villages. It's the *perioikoi* who deal with trade and outsiders, leaving the Spartans free to fight. Even if you went to Sparta, you're unlikely to have much contact with the Spartans, since they keep themselves to themselves.

They're pretty much cut off from contact with the outside world too. They don't even have a system of coins, unlike other city-states. Instead, they simply barter, or trade, goods.

GOVERNMENT & POLITICS

CRADLE OF DEMOCRACY?

Greece is often called the birthplace of democracy, but you may not recognize the original baby. Brought in by Cleisthenes, leader of Athens, in 506BC, it comes from the Greek words for "people" (*demos*) and "rule" (*kratos*). But the only people who can vote are citizens: free men with Athenian parents. Women, slaves and foreign residents are all excluded from the polls.

LOCAL GOVERNMENT

Cleisthenes also split Athens and the surrounding areas (collectively known as Attica) into groups to make it easier to govern them:

ATTICA

was divided into hundreds of small communities called *demes*.

These *demes* were organized into 30 large groups called *trittyes*. There were...

10 groups on the coast...   10 in the city (Athens)...   and 10 in the country.

The 30 *trittyes* were then split into 10 tribes called *phylai*. Each tribe (*phyle*) was made up of 3 *trittyes*: 1 from the coast, 1 from the city and 1 from the country.

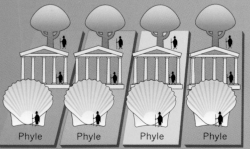

Phyle   Phyle   Phyle   Phyle

THE COUNCIL & ASSEMBLY

New laws and policies are drawn up by the Council of 500 citizens (made up of 50 men from each of the 10 *phylai* or tribes). Councillors are elected annually and each tribe takes a turn running the state day-to-day. Any proposed laws are debated by the Assembly, where every citizen has a right to speak and vote.

The Town Council

The Council meets in a round building called the Tholos.

The building is manned 24 hours a day in case of emergencies.

If you want to see Greek democracy in action, go along to the hill called the **Pnyx**. The Assembly meets here about every ten days. Not only are all citizens entitled to take part, 6,000 of them are needed for a meeting to take place at all. If too few people turn up, police are sent out to round up more voters. (Don't you get carried away and try to vote though. You'll be thrown out.)

SOLDIER POLITICIANS

The most important men in the government are *strategoi*. Basically military generals, ten are elected annually, one from each tribe. They have the job of implementing policies approved by the Assembly. But they're not all-powerful: they must answer to the Assembly for their actions and any money spent.

ANACHRONISTIC ARCHONS

You may also come across the nine *archons*, also elected every year. They used to have immense power, but, these days, they mainly take part in ceremonies. Three of them, however, still have special responsibilities:

The Polemarch Archon

In charge of offerings and special athletic contests held for men killed in war, he also deals with the legal affairs of foreign residents (known as *metics*).

The Basileus Archon

He presides over law courts; arranges religious sacrifices and renting out temple land; and organizes festivals and feasts.

The Eponymous Archon

He finds money men to finance the music and drama festivals and takes charge of inheritance lawsuits, plus the affairs of heiresses, orphans and widows.

OSTRACISM

The Athenians don't simply throw rotten eggs at politicians they're not pleased with. They banish them. Citizens meet in the Assembly once a year to vote politicians out. Everyone writes the name of the person they want kicked out on a broken piece of pot called an *ostrakon*. If a politician has more than 600 votes cast against him, he must leave Athens for 10 years.

POLITICAL GAFFE

Once, a citizen came up from the country to take part in the ostracism vote, but he couldn't write. So, he asked the stranger standing next to him to write down the name of the man he wanted banished. Unfortunately, the man he asked was the man he wanted banished...

FOREIGN POLICY

Ever since the Greeks defeated the Persians in 479BC, they've been waiting for the revenge attack. In preparation for this, various Greek states led by Athens have grouped together to form a league. The first meeting was on the island of Delos in 478BC, so they called themselves the Delian League. Members have agreed to provide ships and money for a navy, and to defend each other's territories in times of war.

THE ARMY

FROM HORSES TO HOPLITES

Originally, the most important part of the Greek army was the cavalry. And, as soldiers had to provide their own horses and weapons, it was made up of wealthy men. Foot soldiers were drawn from the poorer ranks, so their weapons were pretty makeshift too. But recent years have seen the rise of *hoplites*, an elite class of foot soldiers who are much better trained and equipped.

EQUIPPED FOR BATTLE

Early hoplites wore a solid bronze body protector, but – as you need to be flexible to win a fight – modern versions combine bronze with leather. Leg guards are also made of bronze and the whole ensemble is protected from neck to thigh by a bronze and leather shield. A hoplite's main weapon is a long spear backed up by a short iron sword. It's all very expensive and paid for by hoplites themselves.

A 3m (10ft) spear of solid bronze

The body protector, called a cuirass

Leg guards, known as greaves

Iron sword with wooden handle

KEEP IT UNDER YOUR HAT

The helmet of the moment is the *Thracian*, made of bronze and horsehair, with long cheek pieces. Helmets have always been bronze, and usually adorned with horsehair crests, but there have been changes along the way. You might spot a couple of the older designs (shown below) in a march or parade. They're worn by die-hards who refuse to give in to current trends.

Helmets past and present

Later Corinthian helmet

Chalcidian helmet

Thracian helmet

AUXILIARIES

Men who can't afford the rig out of a hoplite act as back-up. They form lightly armed auxiliary units, made up of archers, stone slingers and *psiloi*, who fight with stones, clubs or whatever else is at hand.

CALL UP

Every state has its own way of raising an army. In Athens, there's the "List": men go on it at 20 and are called to active duty if there's a war. Men between 50 and 60 go onto a reserve list, to be called on in an emergency. Each of the ten tribes provides a commander, known as a *taxiarch*, and a *strategos* (general), who is elected by the Assembly. Each tribe also provides enough soldiers for one regiment.

BATTLE PLANS

Soldiers in early armies fought one-on-one. Hoplites fight in formation which needs training, discipline and above all timing. To keep them in step, a piper plays them into battle. Soldiers form a block, or *phalanx*, eight rows deep.

In battle, opposing phalanxes charge together, pushing against each other until one gives way. If a man at the front is injured or killed, the soldier behind takes his place. Each soldier is covered by his own shield and that of the man on his right.

Soldiers on the far right are most vulnerable – so that's where a smart general will attack.

RUNNERS

Certain soldiers from Thrace called *peltasts* try a different tactic. They fire javelins into the phalanx to break it up, then pick off hoplites one by one. Younger, fitter hoplites known as *ekdromoi* are used to chase off these peltasts.

BACK IN THE SADDLE

As hoplites went from strength to strength, the role of the cavalry diminished. But soldiers on horseback will soon make a come back. Not only are they useful scouts, they're handy for breaking up an enemy phalanx.

UNDER SIEGE

A popular tactic is to lay siege to a city, surrounding it with an army and allowing no one in or out. The idea is to starve the city into submission – eventually. Of course the risk is that the army laying siege will also starve – or die of boredom.

A siege tower

An alternative is to storm the walls and a variety of weapons are available. (The following might look like a guide to medieval warfare, but the Greeks were there first.) Towers protect soldiers as they scale walls and, from the ground, catapults fire arrows and hurl rocks.

Then there's the ram. This is a huge tree trunk suspended on ropes and housed in a wooden case on wheels. It's rolled back and forth by soldiers.

Battering ram

In a variation on the ram, fire is sprayed on enemy buildings from a swinging cauldron.

Air is pumped down a hollow tree trunk to feed the fire.

THE NAVY

STICK YOUR OAR IN

The boats you'll be sailing rely on sails and the wind to propel them. This is no use in war. You can hardly say to an enemy commander, "Don't attack today. We're waiting for a decent wind." So, Greek warships have both sails and oars. At first, ships simply had a row of rowers, one down each side. But, since the more oarsmen you have, the faster you'll go, the latest addition to the Greek navy is the *trireme*, with three rows of oarsmen on each side.

THE TRIREME

A trireme's two great strengths are its speed and the fact that it's easy to steer. Assuming all oarsmen are rowing in sync, it's a quick job to start, stop or turn. They can row a boat into battle at up to 15km (9 miles) an hour — far faster than sails can ever manage. But triremes are not without drawbacks, being unsafe in storms and with limited space on board. Even so, they're the most successful and powerful warships in the Mediterranean.

A trireme

CAPTAIN & CREW

Triremes can carry a crew of up to 200 men, of whom all but 30 are rowers. The rest are officers, deckhands, archers and soldiers. Rowers sit in tiers (shown below). The crew is made up of professional sailors and free men, mostly recruited from the poorer classes.

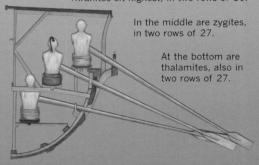

Thranites sit highest, in two rows of 31.

In the middle are zygites, in two rows of 27.

At the bottom are thalamites, also in two rows of 27.

The captain (*trierarch*) is a rich man chosen by the city to pay the ship's running costs for a year. He also usually pays someone else to go to sea in his place.

Wooden mast and linen sail

Sails and masts are lowered onto the deck before a battle.

Ships are steered from oars at the stern (back).

The prow (front) has a ram for sinking enemy ships.

Each oar is over 4m (14ft) long.

SEA WARFARE

At the start of most sea battles, the fleets face each other in two lines. Originally, oarsmen went all out, rowing as hard as they could, and rammed the enemy ship. If the ship didn't sink, at least it would be left in a bad way. Archers then fired arrows at the trapped enemy crew and soldiers went on board to finish them off in hand-to-hand combat.

The newest triremes, however, are light enough and fast enough for more daring tactics. A trireme's captain can now try to attack enemy ships from an unexpected angle – especially the sides and stern (back).

Four ways to sink a ship

1 Sweep around the line of enemy ships and attack from behind

2 Swerve in at the last moment, sweep past the enemy ship and break its oars

3 Swing to the side at the last moment, smashing into the enemy's side

4 Dart through a gap in the line of ships, wheel around and attack from behind

A trireme caught in a storm

Triremes are much less stable when the mast and sails are up.

Trierarch wishing he'd stayed at home

Steering the ship using an oar, which works like a rudder

Captain

There's no room on board for cooking or sleeping facilities, so boats must land each night.

These oarsmen are shown clothed. Don't be shocked if you join a boat and find a crew of naked rowers.

GODS & GODDESSES

LEGENDARY LIVES

You won't get anywhere in Ancient Greece without some knowledge of the Immortals, the gods and goddesses who rule mortal lives. They're as familiar to the Greeks as their own families – and just as temperamental. Many stories are told to explain their personalities and let you know how to please (or avoid angering) them.

IN THE BEGINNING...

...*Gaea* (Mother Earth) arose out of chaos. She had a son, *Uranos* (Sky), whom she then married. They had dozens of children, including fourteen known as the Titans. One of these, *Cronos*, later deposed his father and married *Rhea*, his sister. (Different rules apply to the gods.)

Their youngest son, *Zeus*, followed family tradition, deposing his father and marrying his sister *Hera*. He led his brothers and sisters against their aunts and uncles, the Titans, and ruled from their new home on Mount Olympus. This earned them the nickname, the Olympians.

A WHO'S WHO OF GODS

Zeus: king of the gods, married to Hera. Theirs is a tempestuous relationship and he's had various flings with mortal women. His symbols are a thunderbolt, an eagle and an oak tree.

Hera: wife (and sister) of Zeus and protector of women and marriage. She's a beautiful but proud and jealous goddess, spending most of her time punishing the unfortunate mortals Zeus takes a fancy to. Her symbols are a cuckoo, a pomegranate and a peacock.

Poseidon: brother of Zeus and ruler of the sea. He lives in an underwater palace and is thought to cause earthquakes, hence his nickname, "Earth-shaker". His symbols are a trident (three-pronged fork), dolphins and horses.

Hestia: goddess of the hearth and the most level-headed of the gods. There's a shrine to Hestia in every Greek home. She's gentle and pure, and keeps out of her relatives' constant quarrels.

Demeter: goddess of the plants, whose daughter Persephone was kidnapped by Pluto. Her search for Persephone led her to neglect the plants, causing winter. When Persephone returned, she brought spring and summer with her. Demeter's symbol is a sheaf of wheat or barley.

Ares: son of Zeus and Hera and god of war. He's young, strong and handsome but with a violent temper – not helped by the fact that he's constantly looking for a fight. His symbols are a burning torch, a spear, dogs and vultures.

Eris & **Hebe**: daughters of Zeus and Hera and very different sisters. Eris is goddess of spite – vengeful and troublesome – while Hebe is cupbearer to the gods.

Hephaestos: son of Zeus and Hera, he's a blacksmith whose forge stands beneath the volcanic Mount Etna on Sicily. He built his father's golden throne, and the shield which causes thunder and storms when shaken. He's the patron of craftsmen and husband of Aphrodite (not as great as it sounds).

Aphrodite: goddess of love and beauty, she may be married to Hephaestos but she's in love with Ares. Born in the sea, she rode to shore on a scallop shell. She's a real charmer, thanks largely to her golden belt which makes her irresistible. Her symbols are roses and doves, plus sparrows, dolphins and rams.

Artemis: the moon goddess, her silver arrows deliver plague and death, though she's a healer too. She protects young girls and pregnant women and, although she's mistress of wild animals, she's also a great hunter. Her symbols are cypress trees, deer and dogs.

Apollo: god of sun, light and truth and twin brother of Artemis. He's also the god to turn to for anything connected with music, poetry, science and healing. Apollo killed his mother's enemy, Python the serpent, when it took shelter in a shrine at Delphi. He then took over the shrine to be his oracle. His symbol is the laurel tree.

Hermes: as an impudent child and always up to mischief, he stole cattle from Apollo. But Apollo forgave him when Hermes gave him a lyre (a little like a guitar) he'd invented. To keep him out of trouble, Zeus made him the messenger of the gods. You might like to remember he's also the patron of tourists (and thieves). He wears wings on his hat and shoes, and carries a staff.

Dionysus: god of wine and fertility, he roams the countryside with his followers and gets to sit on Mount Olympus when Hestia leaves.

Athene: daughter of Zeus and Metis (a Titan). She sprang from Zeus's head fully armed. Goddess of wisdom and war, she is also, of course, the patron of Athens. Her symbols are an owl and an olive tree.

Pluto: ruler of the Underworld, the land of the dead. He guards his subjects jealously, rarely letting any return to the land of the living. He also owns all of the precious metals and gems on Earth.

Pluto in his chariot

Asclepius: son of Apollo, god of medicine and, if you believe the story, so good it killed him.

Asclepius learned medicine at the fetlock of his guardian, a centaur (half-man, half-horse). Athene then gave him two bottles of blood: one killed all it touched but the other revived the dead.

It meant that Asclepius cured one too many patients. Pluto told Zeus he was losing too many clients and Asclepius was killed. He was later made into a god by a guilty Zeus who was trying to make up.

DEATH & THE UNDERWORLD

THE FINAL JOURNEY

Greeks believe when they die their souls go to an underground world, only part of which is hell. Those who have led worthy lives end up in a place of happiness and eternal sunshine. They call this underworld Hades and believe it's ruled by Pluto.

FOUR STEPS TO PARADISE

Charon, the ferryman

2. You pay Charon, a ferryman, to take you across the river to the entrance of Hades. (If you haven't been buried with money, you'll be stuck on the bank forever.)

Hermes

1. Hermes, messenger of the gods, guides your soul to the River Styx, which divides the worlds of the living and the dead.

Cerberus

3. Skirt past Cerberus, the three-headed guard dog who keeps the living out and the dead in.

At the crossroads

4. Arrive at the crossroads of your death, where your life is judged. If you've been really good, you'll go on to the sunny Elysian Fields, to spend eternity singing, dancing and generally enjoying being dead.

THE ALTERNATIVES

Asphodel Fields

Those who haven't been especially good or bad end up in a boring place named the Asphodel Fields. (Imagine being grounded forever.)

Tartarus

But souls who have been wicked or cruel are sent to Tartarus, where they face being punished forever.

THE CHOSEN FEW

People who were part of a Mystery Cult have the option of rebirth. If they reach the Elysian Fields three times, they get to the Isle of the Blessed, a place of everlasting joy.

FUNERAL RITES

Getting the rites right is vital if the dead person is to reach Hades. First, the body is washed, doused in fragrant oils and dressed in white. Then it lies on display for people to pay their respects. Mourners wear black and women cut their hair as a sign of grief. On the day of the funeral, a coin is placed in the dead person's mouth to pay Charon, and the body is taken to its tomb, along with family, friends, musicians and professional mourners.

If you're out early, exploring, you may come across a funeral procession. Most set off before dawn for cemeteries outside the city. Don't be upset by the extreme emotions on display. This is a culture not afraid to show grief, with wailing, ripping of clothes and tearing of hair.

R.I.P.

Bodies are buried in the family plot or cremated. The rich are buried in elaborately carved stone coffins. Some even build tombs like small temples to hold them.

Tombs often display a stela, a portrait of the dead person.

FAMILY LIFE

A WOMAN'S PLACE

As you can't have failed to notice, women, particularly from the upper classes, are mostly stuck at home. A girl marries at fifteen, usually to a groom twice her age, taking money and goods from her dad to her new husband. This stays his unless they divorce, in which case wife, money and goods are sent back to Dad.

WEDDING BELLES

The day before her wedding, a girl burns her toys to show she's no longer a child. On the day itself, she dresses up and both families feast and make sacrifices – in their separate homes. The bride only goes to the groom's house that evening (in many cases, the first time they meet). It's only on the following day that families get together for feasting and presents.

TILL DIVORCE DO US PART

For a man to divorce his wife, he simply says as much in front of witnesses. For the woman it's much harder. She has to find an archon who agrees to act for her. In any event, she keeps only what she brought to the wedding from her father. And, whatever the situation, she must leave her children behind.

A WOMAN'S WORK

A Greek wife lives a similar life to a medieval lady in her castle. She looks after the children, stores and household finances; ensures the house is clean and that meals are on time and nurses sick family members. She also spends much of the day spinning and weaving the cloth that makes everyone's clothes.

ALL WORK & NO PLAY?

In some ways, the richer you are, the less fun you have. Wealthy women can only go to festivals and funerals – strictly chaperoned – or enjoy a rare dinner party with suitable female friends. Poorer women without slaves may have to shop and fetch water for themselves, but this gives them ample opportunities for a chat with friends in the market or by the public fountain.

MAD ABOUT THE BOY

In Ancient Greece, male babies are prized far above Rubies (or Helens or Jocastas). This is mainly because, as girls cannot inherit or own property, boys are more likely to support their aged parents. There are cases of fathers rejecting baby daughters and abandoning them. Some cities have specific places to leave unwanted babies, who are then brought up as slaves.

SCHOOLS & LEARNING

BOYS' SCHOOL

Since the purpose of education is to produce good citizens, only boys go to school. Girls are disqualified from citizenship by being girls. The luckier girls are taught at home by their mothers (assuming their mothers can read and write). All schools charge fees, so only boys with wealthy parents can attend.

3 SCHOOLS OF THOUGHT

Rather than learn everything at one school, boys go to a different school for separate subjects. At the first, a *grammatistes* teaches reading, writing and mathematics. The main difference you'll notice from today's classrooms is that instead of exercise books and calculators, boys use waxed boards and an abacus.

At the second school, boys learn poetry and music (including how to play the lyre and pipes), from a *kitharistes*. Dancing and athletics are taught by a *paidotribes*, who takes the boys to a *gymnasium* (training ground). Boys are usually accompanied to and from each school by a *paidagogos*. This paid chaperone keeps an eye on them during lessons too.

Boys start school at seven years old and continue to go until they're eighteen, when they begin military training. There's no higher education as such, but teachers known as *sophists* travel around teaching public speaking.

I HAVE AN IDEA!

If your heart sinks at the thought of a physics or history lesson, blame the Greeks. Not so long ago when people wanted answers to the eternal questions, they turned to the gods. But, from about the 6th century BC, Greek scholars have sought more practical explanations. They do this by closely observing the world around them. Their discoveries will form the basis of much that you learn in the 21st century.

Astronomy: an astronomer named Aristarchus has turned astronomy on its head by declaring that the Earth revolves around the Sun. Most Greeks believe the opposite.

History: the Persian Wars (shh! don't mention them) showed how useful it was to know all about your enemy. This has led to a mania for note-taking by the Greeks about their own lives and others.

Mathematics: new rules are being constantly introduced, including Pythagoras' theories on triangles and circles.

Physics: inspiration even strikes in the bathroom. Archimedes was taking a bath when he noticed that the water overflowed as he got in. Seeing this, he realized that an object displaces its own volume of liquid, enabling him to calculate an object's volume.

Archimedes taking a bath

CLOTHES & FASHION

A FOLD OF FABRIC

The key to Greek dress is simplicity: a rectangular piece of material draped over the body as a cloak or tunic. These cloth rectangles aren't due to a lack of imagination. It's simply that they're the easiest shape to produce on a loom. Wool or linen are used most often, though the rich splurge on silk or even cotton. (Cotton is expensive because it's imported from India.)

HIS...

In Ancient Greece it's the boys who get the chance to show off their legs (and tan). Young men choose either kilts or thigh length tunics, leaving ankle-length tunics for the old and rich. Craftsmen and slaves wear even less, often just a loincloth. Many men, especially philosophers, also wear a *himation* (a rectangular wrap), either over their tunics or on its own. For travel or riding, the short cloak (*chlamys*) is popular.

Tunics are sewn up the sides and fastened on the shoulders.

The chlamys is fastened with a brooch.

The himation: simply wrap and go.

The younger you are, the higher your hem.

...AND HERS

Women wear a single, floor-length piece of cloth called a *chiton*. For those who like to vary their outfits, there's a choice of two: the *Doric* or the *Ionic*. Both are fastened with brooches or pins, and a belt is often worn around the waist. Women wear himations too, though theirs can be anything from a gauzy scarf to a full cloak.

Doric style: folded over at the top, then wrapped around the body with sides left open

Ionic style: fastened along the arms at intervals

Cloaked in a himation and ready to go out.

FASHION PARADE

Like everything, fashion goes in circles. Highly patterned tunics and clinging materials – recently a fashion no-no – are coming into their own again. To be at the forefront of this revival, wear bright, patterned tunics in the finest cloth you can afford. If money's no object, you can even find tunics with gold ornaments sewn into them.

FROM TOP...

Men have short hair and most have neatly-trimmed beards too. If you happen to pass a barber's shop, take a look at the shaving tackle. You'll see why 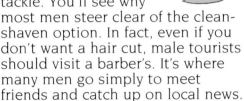 most men steer clear of the clean-shaven option. In fact, even if you don't want a hair cut, male tourists should visit a barber's. It's where many men go simply to meet friends and catch up on local news.

Girls, of course, aren't allowed in, but most women grow their hair long anyway. It's always worn up and held in place with ribbons, scarves or nets. The only exceptions are slaves and women in mourning, whose hair is cut in a short bob. And, bad hair day or not, everyone wears hats outside to protect against the sun.

...TO TOE

Shoes are available, though most people opt to go barefoot. If the ground is too hot for your feet, you can pick up a pair of leather sandals at the market.

For a longer trip, and particularly if you're thinking of riding at some point, you might like to try a pair of calf-length boots for size. These are much sturdier than sandals, but far too hot to wear around the house.

COSTUME JEWELS

Both men and women wear decorative jewels of some sort: brooches, bracelets, necklaces, earrings or rings. There's something to suit every pocket too: gold, silver and ivory pieces for the rich; bronze, iron, lead, bone and glass for the poor. Each piece is elaborately carved and sometimes has enamel set into it. Precious stones, though, won't be used for some years.

Gold earring with a head also wearing earrings

COSMETICS

Greek women are as concerned about their appearance as 21st century girls, and you'll find a huge array of cosmetics and face creams on sale. Eager as you might be to experiment, you'd be wise to stick with toiletries from home. Not only are the creams and face-packs for improving complexions unpleasantly smelly, the basic ingredient of face powder is the highly toxic powdered lead.

An unsuspecting Greek babe finishing herself off – literally – with toxic powder.

MYTHS & LEGENDS

BACK TO THE FUTURE

The Ancient Greeks are great storytellers, using tales of myth and magic to explain the often unbelievable world around them. Legends also tell the exploits of famous heroes in their history. Don't be surprised if some stories seem familiar. Even in the 21st century, writers look back to Ancient Greek tales for inspiration and plots.

PANDORA'S BOX

Zeus created the very first woman in the world out of clay and named her Pandora. He gave her a wonderful box, but forbade her to ever look inside. He must have known what would happen. One day, Pandora's curiosity got too much and she lifted the lid. Out flew all the bad things of the world: sins, sickness and death. But people weren't left in total despair, for the last item to fly from the box was Hope.

CHANGING SEASONS

Demeter, goddess of the harvest, had a beautiful daughter, Persephone. When Pluto saw her, he fell in love. Since she refused to live in the Underworld, he kidnapped her. Demeter was devastated and the crops went to ruin. Finally, Pluto compromised: he'd only keep Persephone for six months a year. When Persephone is with her mother, the sun shines and crops grow. But when autumn arrives, you know the reluctant Persephone is back with her hubby in Hades.

REACH FOR THE STARS

The great inventor Daedalus built a maze called the Labyrinth on Crete, to house the monstrous Minotaur. Having fallen out with the king, Daedalus had to flee. He and his son Icarus flew to freedom on two pairs of home-made wings (made of wax and feathers). But Icarus flew too close to the sun. The wax melted, his wings fell apart, Icarus fell into the sea and drowned.

THESEUS & THE MINOTAUR

Once a year, 14 Athenians were sent to Crete as monster food for the Minotaur. Theseus, prince of Athens, decided to stop the custom. He swore to return under white sails if he was successful. In Crete, he killed the Minotaur, and escaped its maze using a ball of thread – thanks to an adoring princess who left Crete with him. But Theseus then dumped her on an island. To punish him, the gods made him forget his promise, and he sailed home under black sails. His father, Aegeus, thought Theseus was dead and threw himself off a cliff in despair.

PARIS & THE TROJAN WAR

It all began with a beauty contest and the prize, a golden apple. Because three goddesses couldn't agree who was the fairest, a shepherd called Paris (really a Trojan prince), was asked to decide. He chose Aphrodite, who promised him the most beautiful girl in the world as his wife. But this was Helen, who was already married – to the King of Sparta. Paris took Helen anyway, angering the Spartans and triggering a ten-year war with Troy.

DEFINITIONS

THE ODYSSEY

After a decade spent fighting the Trojan War, the Greek king Odysseus could finally head home. But his ships were blown off course and he spent another ten years at sea. By the time he reached his palace, all of his men were dead and other princes were after his crown, not to mention his wife Penelope. Odysseus, who was pretty fed up by this time, killed them all and took back his kingdom.

PERSEUS & THE GORGON

Perseus, a son of Zeus, was told to kill the gorgon, Medusa. Not only did she have snakes where other people have hair, her glance turned men to stone. Athene gave Perseus a mirror so he didn't have to look directly into the gorgon's deadly eyes. Perseus managed to kill Medusa and gave her terrible head to Athene, who stuck it on her shield. (Which shows that, even where gods are concerned, there's no accounting for taste.)

JASON & THE ARGONAUTS

Jason was a prince who was denied his throne by Pelias, his wicked uncle. Pelias sent Jason to fetch the Golden Fleece, a gold sheepskin which hung far away and was guarded by a dragon. Jason set sail in a ship called the Argo, along with his crew, the Argonauts. Like all Greek heroes, Jason was triumphant, albeit aided by the gods and an adoring princess (Medea, who even killed her brother to help him).

acropolis: fortified hill top
agora: market and meeting place
amphora (plural: *amphorae*): large, two-handled pot which holds liquids
andron: men's dining room in a house
aristocrat: rich landowner
cella: main room in a temple
chiton: woman's dress
chorus: actors who speak in unison
citizen: free man with the right to vote
Delian League: alliance of Athenians and others, formed to fight the Persians
democracy: political system in which all citizens have a say in running their state
Elysian Fields: heaven
grammatistes: teacher
gymnasium (plural: *gymnasia*): sports hall
gynaeceum: women's quarters in a house
Hellene: name Greeks give themselves
herm: statue of Hermes guarding a home
hetaira (plural: *hetairai*): woman who entertains men at dinner parties
himation: cloak or shawl
hoplite: heavily-armed foot soldier
Immortal: god or goddess
krater: large vase holding wine and water
mystery cult: religious cult
ostracism: vote to banish politicians
Peloponnesian League: alliance of Sparta and others formed to fight Athens
philosopher: scholar who questions the world around him
relief: sculpture on stone panel
rhapsode: man who recites poetry
sarcophagus: stone coffin
soothsayer: someone thought able to predict the future
sophist: teacher of public speaking
stoa: roofed passageway with columns
Styx: river to the Underworld
symposium: dinner party for men
Tartarus: hell
trireme: powerful warship with three tiers of rowers on each side
Underworld (Hades): kingdom of the dead

MEN (& WOMEN) ABOUT TOWN

An at-a-glance guide to the most famous (and infamous) politicians, playwrights, philosophers and scientists. Names in **bold** have their own entry in the list.

AESCHYLUS (c.525-456BC): one of the best-known Greek playwrights, he's written over 80 tragedies. Only seven will survive, so catch one if you can. Credited with being the first writer to bring dialogue and action to the stage, his most famous work is the *Oresteia*.

ALCIBIADES (c.450-404BC): Athenian politician brought up by **Pericles**, a brilliant but rowdy man and a troublemaker to be avoided at all costs. His pranks include vandalizing statues.

ANAXAGORAS (c.500-c.428BC): philosopher and friend of **Pericles**, whose theories on the universe will influence many other philosophers. Not only has he realized that the Sun is a ball of flames and the moon merely reflects light, he was the first to explain a solar eclipse.

ARCHIMEDES (c.287-212BC): inventor, mathematician and astronomer, he isn't even born at the time of your visit. But he's worth knowing about, not least because he discovered an important law of physics. Getting into a bathtub, he saw that the overflowing water took up the same space as his body, leading to his excited cry, "Eureka!" (*"I've found it!"*)

ARISTEIDES (c.520-c.467BC): politician and general who is known as "the Just" because he's so good, kind and fair. Particularly remembered for helping to set up the Delian League.

ARISTOPHANES (c.445-c.385BC): famous Greek comic playwright and author of over 40 comedies. If tragedy isn't for you, try one of his shows, including *The Wasps*, *The Frogs* and *The Birds*. (Just don't expect animal documentaries.)

ARISTOTLE (384-322BC): the best-known Greek philosopher, he'll study at the Academy, a school to be run by **Plato**. Aristotle won't just study science, he'll invent a new one. (Your biology lessons are thanks to him.)

ASPASIA (born c.456BC): **Pericles'** partner and mother of his son. Because she isn't from Athens, you'll find plenty of people ready to mock her. But she's beautiful, well-educated and counts **Socrates** as a friend.

DRACO (7th century BC): politician who was appointed to improve the legal system and made it harsher. Even laziness became a crime, and one that was punishable by death. **Solon** later abolished most of these "draconian" laws, however, so you can relax and enjoy a lazy holiday without risk.

EUCLID (lived c.300BC): important mathematician who'll write a summary of his predecessors' mathematical ideas. Some of his theories will still be followed in the 21st century.

EURIPIDES (c.485-406BC): author of tragedies, he'll write over 90 plays and win five first prizes at the Athens Play Festival. Famous for his natural style and showing characters' inner feelings, he's been criticized for creating evil characters. But tourists brought up on comic book heroes and villains shouldn't be bothered by them.

HERODOTUS (c.490-c.425BC): the "father of history", he's the first to establish historical facts and show them as a linked sequence of events.

HIPPOCRATES (c.460-c.370BC): doctor who studies a patient's symptoms, seeking practical causes for illness rather than religious ones. 2,000 years later, doctors will still use his promise to treat patients well (the Hippocratic Oath) upon qualifying.

HOMER (c.8th century BC): poet who recited epic tales from memory. His works include *The Iliad* and *The Odyssey*, following the Trojan War and what happened afterwards.

MYRON (5th century BC): sculptor – look out for his famous statue of a man throwing a discus.

PERICLES (c.495-429BC): powerful Athenian politician, who'll be elected war commander for 14 years on the trot. He's also the inspiration behind the Parthenon temple in Athens.

PHEIDIAS (c.490-c.432BC): artist who began as a painter and now sculpts. You can see his statues of Athene on the Acropolis and inside the Parthenon. But you'll have to go to Olympus to see his masterpiece: a vast statue of the god Zeus.

PINDAR (c.518-c.438BC): the poet laureate of the day, he writes odes to great leaders and sporting heroes.

PLATO (427-347BC): brilliant philosopher and pupil of **Socrates**, he'll set up a school called The Academy and write books on how to run an ideal state.

PRAXITELES (born c.390BC): Athenian sculptor who will become famous for his statues of the gods, and develop a new and delicate style, in contrast to the grand, formal style of sculptors before him. (He will also carve the first nude female statue.)

PYTHAGORAS (c.580-c.500BC): philosopher and mathematician who lived with a large band of followers who have passed his teachings down the generations. His discoveries on right-angled triangles have proved more lasting than his peculiar ban on meat and beans.

SAPPHO (born c.612BC): lyrical female poet, who wrote nine books about love, family and friends.

SOCRATES (469-399BC): philosopher famous for being ugly yet charismatic, his mistake was to point out the government's flaws. Accused of corrupting the young, he was sentenced to death by poison.

SOLON (c.640BC-c.558BC): politician who introduced a more humane legal system and encouraged the development of trade and industry.

SOPHOCLES (c.496-c.405BC): prize-winning author of tragedies, who is pioneering the use of stage scenery and is a politician in his spare time.

THUCYDIDES (c.460-c.399BC): politician and historian who's written one of the first history books.

XENOPHON (c.428-c.354BC): writer and pupil of **Socrates**, he fought for the Persians and Spartans against Athens and was banished to Sparta.

TIMELINE

EARLY HISTORY

From **40000BC**   Hunter-gatherers in Greece.
c.6500-3000BC People start moving to Crete; potters set up shop in Greece and Crete.
c.5200-2000BC Farming takes off.

THE BRONZE AGE

c.2900BC Population booms in Greece; towns are established; metalworkers set up beside potters.
c.2500BC The city of Troy is built.
c.2000BC The first Greeks to speak the Greek language identified in Greece.
c.1900BC On Crete, the Minoans take over.
c.1600BC The Mycenaeans become top dogs in Greece.
c.1450BC Crete and the Minoans are overrun by Mycenaeans who go from strength to strength.
c.1250BC The city of Mycenae fortified; the Trojan War (probably) breaks out.
c.1200BC The Mycenaeans lose some power.

THE DARK AGES

By **1100BC** the Mycenaeans lose everything, including knowing how to read and write.
New style of writing introduced in the Archaic Period.
c.850-750BC The poet Homer is born, lives and dies around now.

THE ARCHAIC PERIOD

c.800BC The Greeks, especially traders, start getting in contact with the outside world.
776BC The first-ever Olympic Games are held in Olympia (probably).
c.740-720BC The Spartans start coming on heavy, conquering the nearby state of Messenia.
c.650BC Tyrants seize power in Greece.
c.630-613BC The Messenians stand up to the Spartans but are knocked back down.
c.621BC Draco comes to power in Athens, laying down draconian laws.
c.594BC The Greeks sigh with relief as Solon becomes archon and undoes most of Draco's work.
508BC Cleisthenes takes over and introduces democracy – of sorts.
500-494BC Greek colonies in Ionia turn against their Persian rulers.
490BC The Persians are defeated at the battle of Marathon.
480BC The Persians beat the Greeks at Thermopylae and the Greeks defeat the Persians at Salamis.
479BC The Persians are finally defeated and kicked out of Greece.

THE CLASSICAL ERA

c.500-336BC Greek art has its Classical Period.

478BC The Delian League is formed by Athens and allies against the Persians.

461–429BC Pericles is the politician of the moment (for 33 years).

460–457BC The Long Walls go up; the Acropolis is rebuilt after the Persian attack leaves only rubble.

449BC The Delian League agrees a truce with Persia.

445BC 30 Years' Peace is declared between Athens and Sparta.

431–404BC Just over a decade later, the Athenians and Spartans are fighting the Peloponnesian Wars.

430BC A plague hits Athens.

421BC Athens and Sparta agree to keep the peace for 50 years. (Sound familiar?)

420BC Alcibiades becomes leader of Athens.

413BC Athens and Sparta are fighting again.

407–404BC Three successive victories for the Spartans. The Long Walls are knocked down; the Delian League is dissolved; democracy packs up and leaves Athens.

403BC Democracy comes back.

399BC War breaks out between Sparta and Persia. Socrates is sentenced to death by poison.

395–387BC Corinth, Athens, Argos and Thebes battle Sparta which is still fighting Persia.

394BC The Spartans lose to the Persians.

394–391BC The Long Walls are rebuilt.

387BC The Spartans lose to everyone else.

338BC Philip II of Macedon conquers Greece. The days of independent city-states are over.

THE HELLENISTIC AGE

336–323BC Philip's son, Alexander, founds an empire which breaks up on his death.

323–322BC The city-states fight for their independence, but don't get it.

323BC on Greek states ruled by descendants of Alex's generals.

202–197BC Philip V of Greece hands the country over to the Romans – not without a fight, but one he loses.

147–146BC Direct Roman rule is imposed on the whole of Greece.

INDEX